Having met Tommy Walker when he was just a toddler, it is particularly gratifying to me to be asked to write an endorsement for his new book. What a blessing for him to have written "He Knows My Name"—a song that has so impacted lives around the world. What a testimony to the grace of God that He allows our humble efforts to make such a profound difference in lives!

I so enjoyed reading the individual testimonies about how God has used Tommy's song. And then what a joy to read Tommy's wise and powerful insight as he comments on the stories. Tommy has created a different kind of devotional here, and I highly recommend it to everyone. No one will fail to be touched by the humanity, the spirituality and the heart of this book.

CHUCK GIRARD
CONTEMPORARY CHRISTIAN MUSIC PIONEER

I love the song "He Knows My Name." The Tommy Coomes Praise Band has recorded this and sung it many times on my crusade platform as well as on my father's. The words and music have touched multiple thousands of lives and hearts around the world. I know that the Lord will use this inspired song to minister to many millions of people in the years ahead.

FRANKLIN GRAHAM
PRESIDENT AND CEO, BILLY GRAHAM ASSOCIATION AND SAMARITAN'S PURSE

Tommy Walker has led our congregation in worship many times over the last several years. What strikes me and everyone who crosses Tommy's path is how much he loves Jesus in a childlike way and how authentically he seeks to worship the Lord. I just want to know and love God and people more whenever I'm around Tommy. This powerful little book is a treasure of real-life stories from a man who humbly surrenders his creativity, mind and heart to the Father.

NANCY BEACH
TEACHING PASTOR AND PROGRAMMING DIRECTOR,
WILLOW CREEK COMMUNITY CHURCH
BARRINGTON, ILLINOIS

Tommy Walker has woven together another God-honoring, soul-filling, jaw-dropping work of praise in *He Knows My Name*. Like a clear, deep pool of beautiful water, it reflects a heart that knows the Father's heart well. Its depths are filled with tears of anguish and praise—both are caught in this vessel for the living God. Thank you, Tommy, for leading us beside the still waters again! And thank You, Lord, for restoring our souls through this work!

WAYNE CORDEIRO
PASTOR, NEW HOPE CHRISTIAN FELLOWSHIP
OAHU, HAWAII

I believe Tommy Walker is one of today's greatest psalmists—a leader of worship whose songs are sung everywhere on Earth. I love Tommy's music—always laden with substance but still speaking with simple profundity to any generation or culture. That's why, knowing him as I do, it delights me that in this book others will meet a man whose life in Christ is visibly pure and genuine, and whose pursuit of God's heart is manifestly constant and deep.

Here, he probes the truths within one of his songs that has been greatly used by the Holy Spirit to touch, teach and transform multitudes. "He Knows My Name" is not only a magnificent song of worship, but it is also a means to discovering Father God's readiness today to breathe His life and love into you.

JACK W. HAYFORD
AUTHOR, *WORSHIP HIS MAJESTY* AND *THE HEART OF PRAISE*
CHANCELLOR, THE KING'S SEMINARY
PASTOR, THE CHURCH ON THE WAY

Tommy Walker has been the Church's troubadour of the real for over 10 years, helping people to be exactly who they are in God's presence. *He Knows My Name* continues in story what began in song—a journey into the personal, pursuing heart of God through the lives God's love has changed.

SALLY MORGENTHALER
AUTHOR, *WORSHIP EVANGELISM*
FOUNDER, WWW.SACRAMENTIS.COM
SPEAKER AND CONSULTANT

Tommy Walker has a gift for worship the size
of Texas and a heart that is bigger than his gift. In these
stories, you will find your story. In this song, you
will hear God singing your name.

John Ortberg

AUTHOR, *EVERYBODY'S NORMAL TILL YOU
GET TO KNOW THEM*

Tommy Walker is an anointed songwriter and
worship leader that God uses in an incredible way.
His song "He Knows My Name" has blessed my life.
I know that you will be blessed, too.

Rick Warren

AUTHOR OF THE BEST-SELLERS
THE PURPOSE-DRIVEN LIFE
AND *THE PURPOSE-DRIVEN CHURCH*
PASTOR, SADDLEBACK CHURCH
LAKE FOREST, CALIFORNIA

He Knows My Name

TOMMY WALKER

Regal

From Gospel Light
Ventura, California, U.S.A.

Regal

PUBLISHED BY REGAL BOOKS
FROM GOSPEL LIGHT
VENTURA, CALIFORNIA, U.S.A.
PRINTED IN THE U.S.A.

Regal Books is a ministry of Gospel Light, a Christian publisher dedicated to serving the local church. We believe God's vision for Gospel Light is to provide church leaders with biblical, user-friendly materials that will help them evangelize, disciple and minister to children, youth and families.

It is our prayer that this Regal book will help you discover biblical truth for your own life and help you meet the needs of others. May God richly bless you.

For a free catalog of resources from Regal Books/Gospel Light, please call your Christian supplier or contact us at 1-800-4-GOSPEL *or* www.regalbooks.com.

Rights for publishing this book in other languages are contracted by Gospel Light Worldwide, the international nonprofit ministry of Gospel Light. Gospel Light Worldwide also provides publishing and technical assistance to international publishers dedicated to producing Sunday School and Vacation Bible School curricula and books in the languages of the world. For additional information, visit www.gospellightworldwide.org; write to Gospel Light Worldwide, P.O. Box 3875, Ventura, CA 93006; or send an e-mail to info@gospellightworldwide.org

Poems in chapters 1, 10 and 11 written by Eileen Walker
Cover design by David Griffing
Edited by Jerry Walker

Library of Congress Cataloging-in-Publication Data

Walker, Tommy.
  He knows my name / Tommy Walker.
    p. cm.
  ISBN 0-8307-3636-0
  1. Christian life. I. Title.
  BV4501.3.W355 2004
  248—dc22   2004013654

DEDICATION

This book is dedicated to all the orphans
I've had the privilege of meeting in Third World
countries. God hasn't forgotten any of you. You are
His precious ones, and He knows each and
every one of your names.

HE KNOWS MY NAME

I HAVE A MAKER

HE FORMED MY HEART

BEFORE EVEN TIME BEGAN

MY LIFE WAS IN HIS HANDS

CHORUS

HE KNOWS MY NAME

HE KNOWS MY EVERY THOUGHT

HE SEES EACH TEAR THAT FALLS

AND HEARS ME WHEN I CALL

I HAVE A FATHER

HE CALLS ME HIS OWN

HE'LL NEVER LEAVE ME

NO MATTER WHERE I GO

CONTENTS

PREFACE

The inspiration and the title of this book come from a simple song I wrote in 1996. The book took shape as I sent thousands of e-mails to people in countries all over the world, asking them to send me their personal stories of how that song, "He Knows My Name," and most important, how the truths of that song have affected their lives. You will read many heart-wrenching testimonies within these pages, but in the end there is always hope, because God calls us His own and He sees each tear that falls.

THE STORY BEHIND THE SONG

The story of how "He Knows My Name" was written is not very exciting, nor is it very inspirational. Basically, it's a story of just trying to be faithful to do my job. In that way, it is a story of self-discipline. Let's just say, routine discipline stories are usually far from riveting. However, the fruit of the smallest act of discipline and obedience can be quite another story altogether.

When my pastor, Mark Pickerill, wrote a sermon with the title "He Knows My Name," he asked me if I could write a song to go with it. I felt utterly uninspired that day; but out of the discipline of songwriting, which is part of my job description, I dug in and gave it a shot.

I remember thinking as the words and music began to come to me, *Wow, this is the simplest song I've ever written. Maybe it'll work in kids' church.* Well, I went ahead and finished it—something all songwriters struggle to do when something isn't coming out just right. And like a good, obedient, somewhat disciplined worship leader, I taught it to my church—and basically, nothing happened.

But here's where the fruit of discipline comes in. A few months later, the women of my church sang the song at their women's retreat and suddenly God moved. They told me that a sense of the love of God entered the room in such a powerful way that many of them were weeping and experiencing all kinds of inner healing. When I heard this, I thought, *Maybe I should give this song one more try.*

The following weekend, we sang it at church and, sure enough, it happened: People began to weep. But the funny part is, I also began to weep. God was speaking so intimately to me that day, saying, "Tommy, I know your name, too!" By the way, that's a phenomenon that happens to me fairly often, especially when I write songs using Scripture. Many times it is years later that the Lord will touch me in a new and special way through one of my own songs, as if I had nothing to do with composing it. What a gracious way He has of reminding us that when He uses us, it really is *His* strength and ability flowing through us.

"He Knows My Name" became a "regular" at my church and then slowly began to spread to other churches. All these years later, I've watched this song being sung all the way from orphanages in the Third World to packed-out stadiums in America. It has been used as an invitation song in evangelistic crusades in many countries, and it has been used at funerals and weddings. I even had someone prophesy that it would become the modern-day "Jesus Loves Me." We'll see. I've always loved that simple yet profound "children's" song.

In witnessing all the amazing ways that God has used this song, I often think, *What if I had just decided to be lazy that day? What if I had given in to my discouragement and hadn't finished it? Look at the blessing and impact on so many people's lives that would never have happened.*

I guess it's obvious where I'm going with this. Be faithful in the little things—even when it feels like it's such a waste of time. Be disciplined and finish what you've started in those seemingly ordinary moments, and watch the amazing things God can do!

ACKNOWLEDGMENTS

My deepest thanks to all of you who submitted your stories. For some of you this is the only way I will ever be able to say thank-you for your precious testimonies. Even the testimonies that didn't make it in the book have had a profound effect on what has been written. Your contributions have truly made this book what it is. I feel so honored to have had the chance to be used by the Lord with all of you!

To my brother, Jerry Walker—you added so many heartfelt thoughts and words in the midst of your busy life. Only God, and maybe our mom, will ever know how much you gave to this project!

To Regal Books, thanks for believing in me and giving me an opportunity I honestly never, in my wildest dreams, could have imagined.

To all the spiritual influences in my life: my wife, Robin; Mom; Dad; my siblings—Jerry, Bev, Steve, Dale and Janey; Mark Pickerill; A. W. Tozer; Richard Foster and John Piper.

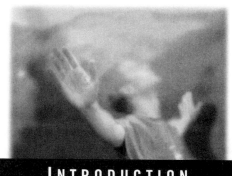

INTRODUCTION

If a Christian book could ever be accused of being "me" centered, it would have to be this one. Every chapter title ends with the word "me." I've never liked Christian books and songs that were "me" oriented. After all, I'm a worship leader and my whole life's calling is about helping people fix their eyes on Jesus and not themselves. That's where real healing and wholeness is found. Right?

All this is true, but before we can ever begin to know and rightfully worship this wonderful creator, our Father God, we must first have our eyes opened to the astounding fact that He not only made us, but He also planned us, intimately knows us, deeply loves us and even flat out likes us. This is where your relationship with God must begin—at the most intimate level imaginable.

To be a blessing to anybody on this earth, you must first be blessed. You can only give what you have received. God wants to deepen, bless and enrich your relationship with Him so that you can give away your relationship with Him to this impersonal, lonely, sorrow-filled, dying world.

This book must be read with your heart and not your mind. The words on these pages are not about acquiring knowledge as much as they are about embracing God's life-changing love! Most of the truths in this book are not new, but they are truths that, through the Holy Spirit, can touch you on the deepest level. Please read every word in an "in the moment" sort of way, as if you were receiving these promises directly from God Himself, for the first time, as intimately and personally as possible.

Drink it in. Soak up every ounce of His ever so close and personal kind of grace, and you and the world around you will never have to be the same!

CHAPTER ONE

HE MADE ME

*For you created my inmost being; you knit me
together in my mother's womb. I praise you because
I am fearfully and wonderfully made; your works
are wonderful, I know that full well.*

PSALM 139:13-14

How Many Children?

Dear God,
How many children do you have?
A million? Billion? Trillion?
He says, "Even more than that!
I have a multitude no one can number—
Ah! And I hold them all in my hand!
Not one is forgotten—I know all about them,
And I supply every need that they have."

Dear Father in Heaven, How rich you must be,
Providing for such a large, growing family!
He says, "My riches are unending—
Beyond comprehending;
Compounding exponentially."

Oh Father God, How wise you must be!
To create such a wide variety
Of people with all different personalities.
Is there no end to your creativity?
He says, "Oh no! I only do originals—
Each one priceless, unique;
And each one expressing a unique
    part of Me."

The first phrase of the song "He Knows My Name" says, "I have a maker," which reminds me of the mind-boggling fact that each one of us is formed by the hand of God. That means we can be assured that we have value and are precious simply and for no other reason than the fact that we are created in His image. Isn't that amazing? We are small, in-process versions of our big creator God. Flowers bloom, waterfalls cascade, cheetahs run fast, and birds fly high; but none of them is made in God's image—only we are. And not only did He make us, but He also made us with a purpose: to reflect who He is and give Him glory with our lives.

I'll never forget watching the birth of each of my four children. How can it be that these little eternal beings, made in God's image, who no one but God had ever met before, just popped out and showed up on planet Earth? To this day I still can't quite comprehend it.

I remember in particular the birth of my third child, Emmie. The minute she saw daylight, she looked around as if to say, "What's going on around here? Who are you guys, and what are you talking about?"

Like the rest of us, she will live her God-ordained years on Earth and I hope, fulfill all the works that God has predestined for her (see Eph. 2:10). Then

Emmie will go on to live forever in worlds unknown to carry out the mystery of God's redemptive cosmic plan. Try to get your brain around that one! Oh, and beyond that, try to fathom the *It's a Wonderful Life* phenomenon: The lives of everyone Emmie meets and interacts with during her lifetime will be altered and influenced in some way because she showed up on planet Earth that hot August day in 1997.

THE GOD WE WORSHIP IS SO OVER-THE-TOP CREATIVE THAT HE DELIGHTS IN MAKING EACH OF US UNIQUE.

Another mind-boggling fact about our creator God is that He makes each one of us different. That's right! The God we worship is so over-the-top creative that He delights in making each of us unique. There are somewhere around 6 billion of His creations on Earth right now, which doesn't even count all the millions of people who have gone before us—and those who are yet to come. Why does He make each one of us different and unique? Well, it's not only because He is creative; but it's also because He is the God of the one lost lamb, the God who took time to visit with social and religious outcasts, the God who had compassion on and healed the blind man. He is the God of the individual! We're not just a huge mass of human beings; instead, we are each unique and we have been created to be unique expressions of who He is. In fact, I believe that if we took the time to get to know this God in an intimate way instead of just imitating one another, we would become even more unique, more interesting, more fun, more peaceful and more joyful; and we would fulfill our true potential, because He is an infinite God with limitless possibilities to express His wonderful, marvelous, fascinating nature.

All this to say, we are fearfully and wonderfully made. Fearfully and wonderfully because we are made in the same image as the most awesome being in the universe—God Himself!

The Heart of the Matter
By Janey Stewart

When Charles Sterling Stewart was born on February 25, 1983, it was a beautiful day in central Florida. Everything had gone smoothly with the pregnancy, and there was no reason to think that anything could go wrong. However, during my labor with him, I had a bad, confusing feeling come over me. I remember telling my husband, Sam, "We need to name him Benjamin instead of Charles. Something isn't right. We must have the wrong name for him." Sam assured me that Charles Sterling Stewart would be his name. Charlie was born at 9:30 A.M. but was immediately rushed to the pediatric intensive care unit because he was extremely blue in color and his heart was beating very fast. In the small hospital in Winter Haven, Florida, they sent for the pediatrician, who notified a pediatric cardiologist, Dr. Alexander, that he had a baby with a heart condition. Arrangements were made to transport Charlie to Shands Hospital in Gainesville, Florida. As it turned out, Charlie was born with a congenital heart defect: transposition of the greater vessels and two large holes in his heart. We were immediately thrown into a world of hospitals, doctors, medical terms, around-the-clock medication, and so on. I am so thankful we decided to stick with the name of Charles; it was significant his entire life. The word to pray for Charlie quickly spread all over the world; we know that God intervened and spared his life. You see, the doctors came to me and told me to hold him for one last time and say good-bye. This baby wasn't going to live past 24 hours because of the gravity of his heart condition. Charlie did live, and his first open-heart surgery was performed at two months of age. One more open-heart surgery occurred when he was almost three years old. Three other pacemaker-related heart surgeries quickly followed. Through all of the surgeries, procedures and hospital stays, we constantly received word that people were praying for Charlie, especially other children. Parents would tell us over and over that their children would remember to pray for Charlie every day because his name was easy to remember. As Charlie grew, he came to love his name. He was proud of his name and always introduced himself to others with a grin, almost as though he knew his name was special.

On February 1, 1996, the Lord decided it was time to take Charlie to his eternal home. Although he had many physical struggles, he was doing quite well on that day when he ran down the street, chasing his little dog. He fell to the ground, his heart beating out of control; he died within four minutes as I rushed him to the hospital. Our grief was unbearable, shocking and overwhelming. We immediately flew to El Paso, Texas, because we were living in Guatemala City, Guatemala, at the time, serving as missionaries. Our family gathered around us to help carry us through those first few days as we buried Charlie and parted with him until heaven becomes home for us all. My brother, Tommy, and his wife, Robin, were among the family members who flew in from California. I remember the soothing comfort I received as Tommy played his guitar and sang song after song of worship to the Lord. When I felt I couldn't even breathe from the overwhelming grief, Tommy would sing worship songs to the Lord and my soul would calm—sweet comfort would come. At Charlie's home-going celebration, Tommy sang the song "He Knows My Name." As Tommy sang the first verse, the words belonged to Charlie:

> I have a maker
> He formed my heart
> Before even time began
> My life was in His hands
>
> He knows my name
> He knows my every thought
> He sees each tear that falls
> And hears me when I call

Charlie had a maker who formed his heart just like He had a plan for Charlie's life and carried Charlie in His loving hands throughout his nearly 13 years on Earth.

Although I will never understand why Charlie had to suffer or why many injustices befall innocent children, I am overwhelmed by God's amazing, redeeming power to take the tragedies and injustices in our lives and turn them into precious, eternal victories. Charlie's Lunch Ministry began as an expression of the grief I felt. My grief wasn't for the fact that I didn't know where Charlie was or even how he was doing but for the empty place in my life here on Earth that had belonged to him. As 1 Thessalonians 4:13 says, we are not "to grieve like the rest of men, who have no hope." But we certainly do grieve. I began feeding hungry children the lunch that I would have prepared for Charlie every day. Today Charlie's Lunch Ministry has grown to 12 feeding centers that provide lunch for nearly 1,000 children on a regular basis. Each month, we serve nearly 10,000 meals. We serve *Charlie's* lunch.

There will never be another Charlie! One thing my sister didn't mention was how Charlie loved to give.

She found that time and again Charlie had given his lunch away at school. My brother-in-law Sam told me once about a time when he took his kids to the store to buy them candy. By the time they were all back in the car, Charlie's siblings had their mouths bulging with gum and everything else because Charlie had already given his candy to them.

Charlie was one of those kids who had a smile that just made you love him and at the same time made you want to love everyone else around him. I don't know how else to say it, but in spite of his defects and imperfections, Charlie was just really good at being Charlie. He wasn't someone special because he was necessarily more gifted than any other child; but Charlie was, and is to this day, an unbelievable gift to so many because he seemed to somehow let you know that he and everyone around him had great significance simply because they were fearfully and wonderfully made by our most significant God!

Only the creator who touched every fiber of Charlie's being when he was being formed in my sister's womb could have given Charlie that heavenly touch of self-worth and selfless love that we all long for.

There have been many times that I have sensed the hand of God touching my life. It is an experience like no other. I remember when I saw the Grand Canyon for the first time. It was certainly a breathtaking experience; but when I was standing there, a lady came and stood beside me and remarked, "Can't you just feel the positive energy?" As she continued to talk to me, I began to discover that she wasn't a Christ-follower. I thought, *She's searching for that heavenly touch just like I am, but there's a big difference.* God comes close to sinful people like her and like me not through nature or energy forces but through the blood of His Son, Jesus, and the gift of His Holy Spirit.

The most primal, instinctual part of who we are as human beings searches the earth for that touch. People do crazy, destructive things to try and find it, but what they're really looking for is the touch from the hand that formed their heart. That's why the very first time our spirits testify with His Spirit (see John 15:26), there is a certain known but not fully known familiarity with His touch.

I'll never forget the first time I sensed God's touch. I was just 11 years old, and a Christian band began to play the old children's song "Jesus Loves Me." My parents told me that Jesus loved me, and I knew I was supposed to love Him, but I had never really had a deep sense of His presence. Suddenly, I sensed this God of my family heritage, the God of the Bible and the God of all human history whisper my name. In my spirit, I heard Him say, "Tommy, I love you, and I have a wonderful plan for your life." I began to weep. I thought, *Who? Little ol' me? You love me and have a plan for my seemingly insignificant life?*

I walked away from that meeting and could honestly say, "He touched me!" The good news is, the God who formed me was the first One to touch me. It is in His creative nature to be ever touching and forming new things in my life and in the lives of all who follow Him!

A God Thought

I believe that God says to the Emmies and the Charlies of the world (that's *all* of us):

> You are My creation, My handiwork, My masterpiece. I'm so proud of what I've done. I see Myself in you and talk about who you are to the angels all the time. Humankind is still only just beginning to discover the intricacies of the human body. I carefully put together every fiber of your being to show

the world My excellence and My majesty. I've put a spirit in you that will live forever and ever. This is something no human mind will ever fully grasp.

Give praise to Me, My daughter, My son, for the wonders I've performed in designing your every part. Take care that you do not compare yourself to anyone but Me. That's right! And I'll tell you why. It is because I made you just the way I wanted you, and I made you with your own limitless potential, just as I am eternal. Therefore, continually set your sights on the greatness of who I am. Stand tall, My child. No other creature in the universe compares to you!

CHAPTER TWO

HE PLANNED ME

Before I formed you in the womb I knew you, before you were born I set you apart; I appointed you.

JEREMIAH 1:5

He chose us in Him [Christ] before the foundation of the world, that we would be holy and blameless before Him, in love.

EPHESIANS 1:4, *NASB*

Nothing is more validating, affirming and comforting than to know that the all-wise creator God—the One who orchestrates the past, present and future—has made us a part of His master plan.

My father is a retired pastor. Years ago, when our church outgrew the rented facility we gathered in, it was time to build our own building. The first thing Dad did was find an architect. I owe my sense of drive and determination to Dad. He always has been a visionary and a planner, and he has greatly inspired me in these ways. I can remember that he and the elders of the church painstakingly thought through every detail that would be needed in the future: a stage; a baptistery; pews; windows and special rooms for babies, toddlers and teenagers. The church also had a Christian school, so they designed areas for sporting events. Every activity that occurred at church had to be thought through and designed. Not only did they think about how everything would have to work to serve the people, but they also had to plan the style and look of the building so that it would help communicate our mission statement.

The building was designed in a casual but beautiful Spanish style. Coming out of the Jesus movement of the '70s, we wanted the church to feel inviting to anyone who walked through the doors. All this to say, this same care toward design is true of you. God, the architect and designer of all designers, took His time and made everything about you on purpose so that

> GOD TOOK HIS TIME AND MADE EVERY-
> THING ABOUT YOU ON PURPOSE SO THAT
> YOU WOULD FUNCTION AND EXPRESS THAT
> IRREPLACEABLE PART OF HIS BODY.

you would function and express that irreplaceable part of His Body. One of my favorite verses in the Bible is "For we are God's workmanship, created in Christ Jesus to do good works, which God prepared in advance for us to do" (Eph. 2:10).

People ask me, "Do you really believe God made you and planned you for specific purposes?" I always say yes! I'll never forget the first time I led worship for a Promise Keepers event. It was at the Silver Dome in Detroit, Michigan. Fifty thousand men attended. When the beginning of the event drew near, I was scared to death. I thought, *What makes me think I can pull off something like this?* I literally wanted to disappear. Suddenly, I sensed the Holy Spirit whispering to me, "Tommy, I made you for this. This is one of those works I predestined for you to do. In your mother's womb, I knit you together for this moment. You can do it; you can do it!" That was an awesome day; but in retrospect it wasn't because of the size of the event. (In fact, I've learned that God's power is not at all dependent on the size of our gatherings.) What was significant that day was that God spoke to my heart in a profound way. He assured me of His plan and calling for my life.

He is speaking to you, too. The most important thing you should celebrate and continue to discover is that God has planned both your strengths and your weaknesses so that you can carry out the specific works He has for you on this planet and beyond!

I encourage you even now to stop and breathe in that sense of validation and purpose from the creator and planner of every aspect of who you are. Just think, God Himself wants you to be a part of history—a part of His story!

My Father's Voice
By Rosanna Fiorazo

I was born and raised in Toronto, Canada, but the rest of my family—my mom, dad, aunts, uncles and grandparents—were born and raised in Italy. Life in a traditional Italian home is a little bit different from life in other children's homes. For example, we had lasagna for Thanksgiving instead of a turkey, but I wouldn't have had it any other way!

I was a very outgoing and joyful child, as well as active and successful in athletics. But there was a very influential person in my life that repeatedly told me, "You were born nothing, you will live nothing, and you will die nothing." For years, I believed him. That man was my father. We had a very tumultuous relationship.

When I became a Christian in 1996, my world turned around for the better. As a new believer, Jesus was everything to me. But life wasn't without its difficulties. When hard trials hit, I began to feel distant from the Lord. I remember thinking, *Maybe He thinks I'm nothing, too.* Every now and then, this lie would creep into my thoughts and convince me that everyone, including God, thought I was invisible. If anyone slighted me, I instantly thought, *They think I'm nothing.*

I began attending Christian Assembly in April 1999 and got involved with the worship team as soon as I could. The very first solo I sang, ironically, was "He Knows My Name." Although I had heard the song several times in the past, it was as if the Lord was speaking directly to me and wanted me to know that He didn't think I was "born nothing"— He assured me I was born with a purpose. I didn't "live nothing," because my life was valuable to Him. And I would not "die nothing," because He was already preparing a place for me in heaven. *Oh Jesus,* I thought, *You really think I'm something.* The elation lasted a short time, and then the enemy attacked me with his lies and tried to convince me again that I was worthless.

I struggled with depression because I always felt so unimportant. I had gone through counseling in an attempt to get through the "daddy wounds." But the entire time I was in counseling, I was filled with anger because I thought I was nothing.

As I grew more and more distant from God, my life felt as though it was spiraling downward. It became more and more difficult to get out of bed in the morning or to even contact friends for some fellowship. Antidepressants didn't help and, of course, more trials came.

I had come across a CD that contained the song "He Knows My Name" and I listened to it. The Lord began to break my heart, and the healing began to take effect. My heart was open to start accepting my acceptance by God. He knew all I had gone through as a child and all I was currently going through. He was just waiting for me to return to the lover of my soul, because He formed my heart and knew every tear that I had ever cried. There would always be open arms longing to hold me and a tender voice whispering, "You are everything to me."

That day came just a few months ago. Father God penetrated my heart with the truth that every trial I had gone through was to build my character for eternity and for the purpose that He has for me on Earth. I crossed the line from worthlessness to being an integral part of God's great kingdom. I thank Him for never giving up on me and for always calling my name during the darkest days of my life. I may not have heard Him call my name, but He kept calling it just the same. He knows my name and He'll never forget it. It's written in the palm of His hand!

Not only did God know you before the foundation of the world, but He also planned for you. He planned your uniqueness, the time in history in which you would be born and His purpose for your life. Married, single, with child, without child, unemployed, employed—take heart, for whatever life circumstances you find yourself in, God has a plan!

Another of my most memorable experiences was when I stayed at an orphanage in the Philippines in 1997. When I, and my group, arrived, about 60 orphans greeted us with a song of welcome and then began to sing songs of praise to the Lord. Then they all began to bow to us and give us some of the most pure, affectionate hugs I've ever received.

Over the course of the next few days there were times when I would purposely sit on a couch in the main room and they would all come around and snuggle up next to me. I remember thinking that to the natural mind, according to "conventional wisdom," nearly every one of these children would be considered an "accident." They were just little kids born in a Third World country—most of them out of wedlock and some out of lifestyles of prostitution and drugs. They weren't planned, right? That's right; by human design they weren't planned, and, in fact, many people would view these little ones as a burden on society. But to God they each have a name and an eternal purpose.

One seven-year-old boy I met at the orphanage was named Jerry. I've been privileged to tell his story in many countries throughout the world. When we first arrived, Jerry introduced himself to me and said, "We're friends, right?" I said, "You bet." The next day he approached me and asked, "What's my name?" I said, "I know your name. It's Jerry." Again he said, "We're friends, right?" I said, "Of course we are!" This conversation would happen two or three times a day, every day, until finally I realized what was happening. Jerry was an orphan in the Third World, living in an orphanage. He could be considered one of the most unknown, forgotten people on Earth, but he just wanted somebody to know his name. Fortunately, I was able to remind little Jerry that though I knew his name, there is one much greater who knows his name and will never forget it—God the Father!

When I tell this story, I always see people touched by it. What I love the most is the fact that this little unknown orphan boy—who just wanted me to know his name—has now had his name spoken and heard in many countries throughout the world. Don't you just love the fact that God loves the underdog? (More about that later.)

Here is a little boy who could certainly seem unplanned according to the world's standards of propriety and significance; but the whole time I was with him and his little buddies, I heard God in my heart telling me how precious each one of them was to Him. Imagine a God who, before He made the stars in the heavens, thought about how much He loved little Jerry and how He was going to use Him to touch people all over Earth. This mystery of God's loving providence brings me such hope! Because if He planned me, then He must want me. And if He wants me, then He must really love me and have wonderful things in mind for my life.

Perhaps God's plan doesn't always appear to be wonderful on the surface, as in Jerry's case, but there is no question that we can affirm, "great and marvelous are Your works, O Lord God" (Rev. 15:3, *NASB*), in and through us from an eternal perspective.

A God Thought

I can just hear the Father saying to Rosanna and Jerry (and to you) these words straight from His heart:

Your life was in My hands before I scattered the stars in the sky. I had you in My master plan so that I could shine my light through you in a way that can be shone only through you. Those voices you hear at night that seem to say, "You're a nobody; you'll never amount to anything," are definitely not from me! They are from the enemy of your soul who plays on your self-doubt and fragile self-esteem. Satan says those things because he knows you are a threat to his plans of death and destruction on this earth. If you just begin to catch a glimpse of how thoroughly and perfectly I have planned your life, then you will stand up and be the history maker I have designed you to be.

CHAPTER THREE

HE KNOWS ME

See, I have engraved you on the palms of my hands.

ISAIAH 49:16

O LORD, you have searched me and you know me. You know when I sit and when I rise; you perceive my thoughts from afar. You discern my going out and my lying down; you are familiar with all my ways. Before a word is on my tongue you know it completely, O LORD.

PSALM 139:1-4

Rejoice that your names are written in heaven.

LUKE 10:20

What's in a name?

Few of us stop to think much about names, except for parents-to-be who scour name-your-baby books. For the most part, we use names to tag people—to label them and differentiate one person from another. We don't think much about the fact that names have deeper significance in identifying or even affirming someone.

I believe our culture's casual approach to names reflects where we are as a society. I'm not a sociologist, but it's easy to spot the difference between the way we usually use and think of names today and the way in which people in the Bible treated names.

In the cultures and times of the Bible, names were taken very seriously. They weren't just a label; they were understood to identify people in terms of their heritage and, sometimes, the circumstances of their birth, and even their character and destiny. Names are one of the most inspiring and revealing ways that God communicates to us who He is: "Wonderful, Counselor, Mighty God, Everlasting Father, Prince of Peace" (Isa. 9:6, *NKJV*).

Even though our modern culture doesn't seem to place the same level of value and meaning on names that we see in the Bible, it's interesting how we respond personally to having our name spoken. When we hear our name or we just think about someone else who knows our name, our hearts are stirred.

It is so interesting to me to see how the lyrics to "He Knows My Name" have touched so many people on such a deep level. We do seem to have a good deal of our identity and self-esteem tied to our name.

Here is how Colin Wiseman (one of the generous people who offered her insights for this book) describes how hearing her name has affected her:

I will always remember "the sound"—the sound of my mother or father calling my name. I remember the sound of them saying my *whole* name. "*Colin Avery Wiseman*, you'd better get in here, *now*!" I knew I was in trouble when I heard that tone and my whole name.

However, I also remember my parents sitting me down, looking at me and saying, "Colin, you can be what you want to be. You just need to follow God and let Him guide you." That soft tone used with my name was so personal and intimate, because they knew me. They cared for my every need and always looked out for my best interest even if I thought I knew better.

Depending on the circumstances, hearing your name can be heartwarming or heart wrenching. One woman—her name is Cindy—cringed at the sound of her name. When she slowly began to realize just how important and irreplaceable she was in God's eyes, her name took on a different meaning to her—one of delight.

Is There Love in a Name?
Anonymously told to Tommy Walker

I'll never forget when the lights finally came on in Cindy's eyes. She had lived under a cloud of darkness, and a lingering sadness hung about her.

She hated her name. Every time she heard "Cindy," it registered in her as "sinning." She felt dirty and shamed at the very mention of her name. Tragically, Cindy had been sexually abused by her father when she was just a child. The pain of that had been buried inside her for more than 30 years.

One day, as she was able to bring all of her pain to the light of God's cleansing love, she felt she heard her heavenly Father speaking her name. She wanted to tell God to stop saying that awful name, but He kept speaking it with such affection and warmth and love. It was as though He began singing her name, like a gentle father would sing to his baby girl as he rocked her in his arms. Suddenly, it was revealed to her that God had chosen her name from before the foundation of the world. Her name was so sweet to Him. It was a name that was like the sweetest song, because it was the name He had chosen for one that He loved beyond words.

God began an incredible healing and transformation in Cindy's life. The dark shadows were replaced with a bright glow. Her testimony before the church spoke of how God had turned the ashes of her life into gold. She felt that everything about her and who she was had been taken away and ruined, but God took all of that and through His love turned her life into something she could celebrate and enjoy.

Names are so important! Hearing our own name always impacts us—whether the impact is positive or negative. I was forwarded an e-mail (origin unknown), about a little boy named Billy, who said, "When someone loves you, the way they say your name is different. You just know that your name is safe in their mouth."

When I was selected for jury duty recently, I went to a courthouse in Los Angeles, where about 200 of us waited in one room to be called. At the beginning and end of the day, role was called over a microphone. Here were all these adults, from all walks of life, and when they heard their name called, it was as if they were in grade school again. A smile would come across their faces and they would shout out, "I'm here!" Many of them would look around to see if anyone had noticed who they were. There is just something about the sound of our names that brings out the child in us.

That experience showed me that our names are important to us, not just in the sense of owning the name we have, but in recognizing *who* knows our name. This can get carried to almost ridiculous lengths when people name-drop. You know, when someone tries to impress you because he or she knows someone who is considered important or famous. When you live in Los Angeles, you hear a lot of name-dropping. People connect their value to who they know, who knows them and who they've worked with. I despise this, because when we name-drop, we're basically saying that our value comes from people and not from God. The truth is, I'm worth something because I belong to Him. I have significance because He's the most significant one of all!

I remember a time when I arrived home and my wife told me that a top executive from a large record company had called and asked to speak to me. I wasn't aware that this person had ever heard of me, much less had any reason to want to talk to me. I felt so valued and affirmed, because someone I thought was so great and powerful knew me!

THERE IS SOMEONE CALLING YOUR NAME RIGHT NOW WHO IS THE MOST FAMOUS, POWERFUL, INFLUENTIAL, WEALTHY, WISE AND LOVING BEING IN THE ENTIRE UNIVERSE—GOD HIMSELF!

While it is certainly a blessing to get calls like that, the inevitable problem is that there comes a day when those kinds of people won't call anymore. One of the foundational issues in this book is that there is someone calling your name right now who is quite a bit more important then a record company executive. It is God Himself—the most famous, powerful, influential, wealthy, wise and loving being in the entire universe! If you can wrap your faith around that, then you will never be the same. In other words, it's not so much who you are but *whose* you are!

I remember years ago doing a concert in a Christian coffeehouse in Hollywood. This coffeehouse ministered mostly to the addicted and homeless in the area. One night after our concert, we met a homeless man named Larry. Larry was very dirty and didn't smell so good. He had a filthy blanket wrapped around him to keep him warm. We decided to go out to eat, and I invited Larry. The restaurant was just around the corner. I'll never forget the minute Larry stepped foot in that place. The manager ran up and told him he had to leave. Immediately, I walked over to her and spoke words that made all the difference, I said, "He's with me." With that, she disappointedly replied, "Okay, Larry, you're in."

I thought, *Wow, what a picture of the gospel!* Without Christ, we are "out," but if we place our faith in Jesus Christ, then someday before the Father He will say, "He's (or she's) with me!" He will identify us by name!

It seems to me that Western civilization (which is becoming more and more the global culture) is sliding down the slippery slope of depersonalization, evidenced in a number of ways but certainly exhibited in the way we treat names. Although it may seem like a small thing, the fact that you take care to remember someone's name and that you cherish the names of those you know will help to reverse the trend toward depersonalization. This trend is degrading and dangerous, because it is not the way God relates to us. The Bible says that God knows us so intimately that "even the very hairs of your head are all numbered" (Matt. 10:30). "See, I have engraved you on the palms of my hands" (Isa. 49:16). Not only does He know your name, but He also keeps your name ever before Him!

I'm talking about this because as we look at history, what has always facilitated the most sinister, heinous evil required depersonalization—thinking of people in groups or categories and building up a bureaucracy to maintain the system. Individual names are not conducive to bureaucracies. That's why, in a monstrosity like the Holocaust, the Jewish people were numbered to identify them. Their names were forgotten.

Think about it; do you find it easier to label a homeless person a beggar than to find out his or her name? When we don't know someone's name, it is much easier to avoid intimacy and all other emotional connections.

Our heavenly Father relates to us not by category or classification or number—"God shows no partiality" (Acts 10:34, *NKJV*)—but by name. He is on the most personal and intimate level conceivable. He knows you just as you are.

Andy Hubert, raised in Panama, says it so well: "When I talk to my Father, I'm not known as customer 99 or request 90210. With all my questions, concerns and worries, my Father is not only concerned with them, but He's also concerned about *me*—Andy. He calls me by my name. What a concept! With a couple billion children the world over, it's wonderful that He knows us all by our names. Thank you for that, Jesus."

I agree with Andy. As I've sung "He Knows My Name" all over the world, the one thing I have found is that when people come to realize that their heavenly Father knows them this intimately and values them this highly—"He knows my name; He knows my every thought; He sees each tear that falls; And hears me when I call"—they begin to shake off the feeling of being alone and unknown.

A God Thought

The simple song "He Knows My Name" proclaims that He, the Almighty, who is also your Father in heaven, knows your name and everything about you. In fact, I encourage you to quiet your spirit, even now, and listen to Him call your name. He says:

Jerry, Linda, Michael, Johnny, Sandy, Susie, David—I've been here all along. I know everything about you, and I love you like no one ever has or ever will. Listen, my child; I am ever calling *your* precious name!

CHAPTER FOUR

HE FORGIVES ME

He was pierced for our transgressions, he was crushed for our iniquities; the punishment that brought us peace was upon him, and by his wounds we are healed.

ISAIAH 53:5

The second line of the chorus of "He Knows My Name" is "He knows my every thought." This is both a comforting and a terrifying line; comforting because it reminds us that He knows and understands what we're going through, and terrifying because He sees the wickedness of our hearts and thoughts. Can you imagine what it would be like if we all had a color TV on our heads to televise our most intimate thoughts to the world? I don't think I would have very many friends, and I don't think anyone would be able to argue that the human race is basically good and getting better. The truth is, we've all fallen short of God's glory (see Rom. 3:23) and are in desperate need of a savior. And not just any savior, but Jesus Christ Himself—the one whose death was prophesied centuries before His birth.

I, like millions of other people, saw the movie *The Passion of the Christ*. I was so moved by the very first thing I saw. The words from Isaiah 53:5 appeared on the screen and told us that Jesus "was pierced for our transgressions, he was crushed for our iniquities; the punishment that brought us peace was upon him, and by his wounds we are healed."

This verse was written 700 years before Jesus died on the cross! Yet it so perfectly explained the film we were about to see. And of course the story is much more than a film. It's the true story that changed human history forever. Behold the man, the chosen Lamb of God—Jesus!

IT WASN'T THE NAILS THAT KEPT JESUS ON THE CROSS, IT WAS HIS LOVE.

There were of course many moving parts in that film. I was reminded that Jesus not only died but was tortured for me. On Good Friday, I took Communion with my wife and kids and told them that when I saw that first nail go through His hand, it pierced the depths of my heart because it felt like that was the point when there was no turning back for Jesus. As soon as I said that, my six-year-old daughter, Emmie, said, "Daddy, it wasn't the nails that kept Jesus on the cross, it was His love." I was speechless. Emmie's words are so true; only the greatest love the world has ever seen could have endured such a feat! And only that kind of love could ever buy the forgiveness that all of us need.

The blessings and promises from the intimate God we have talked about so far in this book are available only because He knew your name when He hung on that cross. He thought of *you*! Remember the two thieves who were on crosses next to Jesus? One thief said, "Jesus, remember me when you come into your kingdom" (Luke 23:42). In other words, remember my name, Lord, and please have mercy on me.

The Ultimate Sacrifice
By Mark McLaughlin

You would never believe that a boy who grew up in a Christian home, attended a Conservative Baptist church every time the doors were open (Sunday morning, Sunday night and Wednesday night), participated in a kickin' youth group in the '70s and even attended a Bible college in the '80s could somehow miss the message of God's grace. But this boy did for 30 years of his life. My name is Mark McLaughlin, and I'd like to tell you my story of how coming to know the God who knows my name changed my life.

I accepted Christ as Savior at an early age and spent the next 20-plus years searching for a reason to be excited about having a relationship with Jesus Christ.

I don't know if I was absent on the Sundays my teachers talked about God's grace or if it was never taught. Perhaps, even through the hundreds of sermons I heard over those years, I just never caught the one on forgiveness. What I do remember is being keenly aware of my sin and my faulty ability to resist it, and I felt that God wasn't pleased with me when I failed to resist it. Sin consumed my Christian life. Either I legalistically avoided it or wholeheartedly did it. My days were spent thinking about how sin lived inside of me.

What baffled me was how truly miserable I was as a Christian when I worked so hard at it. I did all the right things but had nothing to be happy about inside. I wouldn't witness to my friends, because I surely couldn't say to them, "Accept Jesus in your life and your life will become extremely frustrating and miserable!" Not exactly a great selling point for Jesus.

When I was 30 years old, God finally allowed me to understand for the first time what radio commentator Paul Harvey means when he talks about "the rest of the story." I happened upon a radio program in which the speaker was talking exclusively about God's grace. This awakened my spiritual journey and adventure as unanswered questions I had held for years were answered.

I couldn't believe that after all that time I finally had my answer. It wasn't about me and my struggle with sin. Instead, it was all about what Jesus had done for me, and His struggle with sin for me.

Over the course of the next year, my life changed dramatically. My theology was realigned with the truth of Scripture. I unlearned and relearned many things through the eyes of God's grace. It was a wonderful time in my life.

One day, when I was listening to Christian radio, I heard "He Knows My Name" for the first time. I felt like the songwriter had been reading my mail. After many years of searching, I knew I had finally found this personal and intimate relationship with my Father, and the song expressed for me that intimacy.

The song also expressed God's ultimate, sovereign plan to allow me to wait until I was 30 years old to find the relationship I longed for in the refrain, "He sees each tear that falls and hears me when I call." You could fill a bathtub with the tears of frustration, anger and dissatisfaction I wept over those earlier years. But you could also fill another one with the tears of joy I have experienced in the past 14 years. There is nothing that will ever separate me from the personal and intimate love relationship I have with my Father provided by the sacrifice of Jesus Christ for me.

Grace is getting what we don't deserve and getting what we could never earn. In fact, it is an insult to God's gift to us on Calvary when we imply that any of our righteous acts would ever make us good enough to deserve a right relationship with this holy God. To add a little bit to what Mark was communicating in his story, the thing that differentiates Christianity from other faiths is that it is all about responding to what Christ has already done for us, not about what we can do to be good enough to get a thumb's-up from God.

One of the most beautiful things the Cross did for those who believe is that it connected our names with His name. I now have the privilege of bearing His name as a Christian, and He has placed my name on His family tree and in the Lamb's book of life. I can see it now:

PAGE 1:	**PAGE 2:**	**PAGE 3:**
God the Father—the great "I Am" God the Son— Jesus Christ God the Spirit— Immanuel	Apostle Paul Martin Luther Billy Graham Jesse, Pam Rosanna, Charlie Breanna, Tommy Your name . . .	All the unborn babies All the millions of street children in Third World countries (except I think their names will be first)

Wow, what a blessing, what a gift! And all we have to do is lift our arms in faith and say, "Remember me, Jesus; have mercy on me, a sinner. I believe and I receive." What a gracious God we serve!

If you have been searching for the touch and presence of God, feeling far from Him, or have never accepted Christ as your Savior, at some point while reading this book, I encourage you to pray this prayer from the bottom of your heart:

> *Dear Jesus, I believe that You and You alone are the Savior of the world. You're the One who died on a cross for me and rose again so that I could become Your child forever. Please forgive me of my sins and wash me clean of all unrighteousness. I ask You to write [insert your name]—which You've known since before the foundations of the earth—in Your Lamb's book of life. Amen.*

The Bible says in Romans 10:9: "If you confess with your mouth, 'Jesus is Lord,' and believe in your heart that God raised him from the dead, you will be saved." If you sincerely prayed that prayer, welcome to the family of God! You are born again. Now go tell someone. In fact, go tell everyone! Let the whole world know that He made you, He touched you and He has now saved you!

A GOD THOUGHT

I saw your face when they spit on me. I thought of your name when they pierced my side. The Cross wasn't about Me enduring some big religious ritual that had to be performed. It was about you! I did it for you because I loved you, planned you and want you, above all things, in My creation. The power of My love that was demonstrated that day on the cross has the power to change every aspect of your life forever. I built you with one central need, and that is to be accepted and loved. And loved you are! So when you are forgotten and rejected, when you fail and don't succeed, when you feel worried and alone, remember that symbol of torture and grace, My cross. It gave you what you need most—even more than the air you breathe. It gave you My matchless, enduring, life-changing love!

CHAPTER FIVE

HE UNDERSTANDS ME

*For we do not have a high priest who is unable to sympa-
thize with our weaknesses, but we have one who has been
tempted in every way, just as we are—yet was without sin.*

HEBREWS 4:15

*When we were children and fell and skinned
our knees, though our mother couldn't really do
anything for the pain, it sure somehow felt better
after she picked us up and kissed us.*

ANONYMOUS

To be truly known by someone means, at the deepest level, to be understood by that person. Someone may know of you, know some things about you, or know you on an acquaintance level; but the kind of knowing we're talking about here is to be known at the level of understanding. The people to whom we tell our deepest worries, secrets and cares are the ones who understand us and can truly comprehend what we are going through.

The first verse of one of my favorite hymns goes like this: "Man of sorrows, what a name for the Son of God who came, ruined sinners to re-claim! Hallelujah! What a Savior!"[1] It speaks of how Jesus, though being God, humbled Himself and came to Earth to save us and relate to our lives in this crazy world. God's redemptive plan to rescue us from the world, the flesh and the devil, included a very wonderful component: Jesus identified with our human experiences, even our weaknesses, so that we can be assured that He really and truly understands us. Jesus actually went through all the stuff we go through in this life. The Bible says that Jesus learned obedience through suffering (see Heb. 5:8) and that He was tempted in every way as we are yet was without sin (see Heb. 4:15).

Right after Jesus was baptized by John the Baptist, which was the launching of Jesus' ministry, He "was led by the Spirit into the desert to be tempted by the devil" (Matt. 4:1). We read that he experienced severe hunger. At this point, Jesus was vulnerable on a physical level, so the temptation to break His fast in a compromising way was real and compelling. Think about it; Jesus was hungry to the point of starvation. So Jesus had to resist temptation that hit Him on the level of His body—crying out for something to eat—and exercise faith and trust in His Father's best plan rather than allow Satan (and the call of His fleshly body) to confuse and corrupt God's purposes.

Satan went on to tempt Jesus to put God to the test—to act rashly on the basis of presumption rather than on the basis of faith—by leaping off the highest point of the Temple in Jerusalem. This particular temptation also involved power and fame. Jesus again refused to compromise or to disobey God, even though the payoff of giving in to this temptation was so available to Him at that moment that I'm sure He could "taste" it.

The big finale was that Satan enticed Jesus to bow down and worship him. This was the shortcut way, the easy way out of securing something that seemed so good and right—Jesus' dominion over the kingdoms of the world. Now, if you've attentively read the passages of Jesus' suffering on the cross (or have seen the movie *The Passion of the Christ*), you have to appreciate that this was a real temptation for Jesus. But it was contrary to Scripture, and Jesus stood solidly on the promises of God rather than give in to the "glory" of the immediate and the earthly.

In these temptations Jesus faced at the very beginning of His ministry, He was put through the wringer (as He was throughout His ministry, death and resurrection), so there can be no question that He was tempted in every way as we are. In other words, Jesus understands the weakness of your human nature. Even though He did not sin, He knows what it feels like to be enticed by sin and drawn close to the compromises that are all around us. He doesn't just understand you from the viewpoint of being the omniscient, all-knowing God Almighty; He understands you from the experience of having felt what you feel—all of it!

Let's go a little deeper with this. Jesus went *through the process* of experiencing the weakness of the flesh, the pull of the world and the badgering of the devil, for "he learned obedience from what he suffered" (Heb. 5:8). When you think about whether Jesus truly understands you—your painful past, your present troubles, your fears for the future—don't spiritualize it or dilute it. His understanding of you is all the way. Jesus felt, tasted, struggled with and learned from the very same kind of pain, disappointment, weaknesses and challenges that you face. He's been there—physically, emotionally, mentally and spiritually.

JESUS FELT, TASTED, STRUGGLED WITH AND LEARNED FROM THE VERY SAME KIND OF PAIN, DISAPPOINTMENTS, WEAKNESSES AND CHALLENGES THAT YOU FACE.

Now here's the really good part. The Bible says He "always lives to intercede for [us]" (Heb. 7:25) and, "we have one who speaks to the Father in our defense—Jesus Christ, the Righteous One" (1 John 2:1). Jesus sits at the right hand of the Father, praying for you and pleading your case before the throne of God. Right now he's saying something like

"Father, have mercy; forgive and restore our beloved child during this trying time. You and I know that Bob [or Jim or Linda or Jenny or . . .] is but flesh; You and I know that Our Holy Spirit can strengthen, sustain, inspire, empower and raise up this one for whom I died, to fulfill the purpose for which You created him. You know, Father, I don't plan to let a single one of those You have given to me be snatched from My hand. Take a look now and see: The first half of the miracle is in motion. Let's not delay in sending the second half. For I have such compassion on My child. I've been there, done that. I know exactly how he feels right now. Look, look! He's beginning to turn toward us, beginning to reach out in faith. Don't delay; stretch out Your mighty arm to save him! I can't wait to dance for joy as I watch Our redemption, grace and mercy unfold in that precious life and begin touching the lives of those around him!"

Not only does Jesus take on the role of advocate for you with the Father, but He also sings and shouts over you with joy as He directs: "Go, Holy Spirit, go! That's one of my [multitrillion] favorites there! Comfort, console, strengthen, encourage and reassure him [her] that I truly, completely, exhaustively understand what he is going through. But also speak to his heart that it won't be long until he will know as he is known and that this temporary suffering will not even be noticed when compared with the glory that will be revealed in him."

Never forget that Jesus experientially understands the kinds of things you deal with. This is so important to internalize! To put a different spin on an old adage, Jesus knows that suffering *needs* company.

I'm No Statistic
By Natalie Dunbar

Behaviorists and other social scientists tell us that being known—being acknowledged and affirmed—is one of our most basic human needs. However, if you are someone whose upbringing didn't always include that confirmation, then to understand how God the Father could know and love you is virtually unfathomable.

I remember sitting in a circle of single parents many years ago at a dinner sponsored by our church. Weeping along with the rest, I remember a single mom—just like me—who said that whenever she feels forgotten by her family and friends, she remembers the words of a special song, and it reassures her that she is known and loved by the Father like no one else.

It was during those days that I increasingly came to realize that this God—a God that up until then seemed strict and demanding—really does know me. As Psalm 139 says, "You knit me together in my mother's womb" (v. 13). And as the old folks used to say, "God don't make no junk!"

Moving that concept from my head to my heart was an entirely different matter. Trained as a social scientist and working as a journalist, my default response for these kinds of religious declarations was "Prove it to me. I'll believe it when I see it." I relied on what I knew science proved to be true. As human beings we have a tendency to attach labels to things and people we don't know or understand. We label partially to make sense of something that is otherwise unknown to us, and many times to help reinforce the boundaries between "us" and "them."

As a student of sociology, I could understand this tendency—what sociologists refer to as the theory of social labeling. But as a divorced, single mom, no amount of understanding could take away the pain of the circumstances I was in or the painful road that got me there.

If this God who claimed that He knew my real name (who I am in Him), and knew that I cried many bitter tears over the treatment I received from those who labeled me, making me a statistic and writing me off as a throwaway, loved me, then why didn't He show Himself? Why didn't He remove the burden and pain of my life and help me to walk upright instead of hunched over in shame?

It took singing "He Knows My Name" over and over for many years before I truly began to understand that there is no place I can go—even to the depths of pain, sin and despair—where He cannot see me, know me and understand me! Moreover, because He is truly my life's director and "All the days ordained for me were written in your book before one of them came to be" (Ps. 139:16), He can—and did—use my suffering for good.

"He knows *my* name." And it is not "throwaway," "misfit" or "loser." It is "princess," for I am a daughter of the King!

"He knows my every thought." My thoughts are not negative, nor do they curse His wonderful creation. Instead, they are made in His image and are becoming more and more shaped into His thoughts, which are precious to me.

"He sees each tear that falls." When I cry out, my tears are not in vain. They do not fall unnoticed and melt away without care. He uses these tears as living waters for His sheep. He has called me to cry over those in the flock who are just like me and to help them go forward to recovery in Him.

"And [He] hears me when I call." My cries do not fall on deaf ears. He is near to me, and through Him I am called—called to go and make disciples (see Matt. 28:19).

As I learn to know the many names of God, He reveals to me what has been planned for my life all along. These days, in addition to being called Mom, I'm also a writer, small-group leader and home owner, among other things.

In the end, though, I am thankful for the many blessings God has bestowed on my son and me, and I am happiest being called "servant." I'm coming to the full realization that He really does know me and that He understands and loves me!

Jesus is like no other God or being who has ever lived. He can sympathize with all of our hurts, disappointments, aspirations and dreams as no one else can. God the Father knew exactly what He was doing when He sent His son to Earth. If Jesus had been born into even the middle class, how would He fully know the pain of the poor? If He hadn't represented ultimate royalty and majesty, He wouldn't have been able to reach out to the privileged and affluent. Only because He was fully God and fully man could He understand what it's like to be tired, tempted, hurt and frustrated. He came from the heights of heaven and lived a humble life on Earth with a humble job and hung out with humble people.

I love the shortest verse of the Bible: "Jesus wept" (John 11:35). It blesses me to know that my God has emotions just like me. He knows what it feels like to hurt and to grieve. He understands all of my experiences.

What a revolutionary, sovereign plan God came up with to come to Earth, dwell with the likes of us and live a perfect life, yet experience everything we experience!

I guess you could call this sovereign plan of God's a sort of support group. Support groups are known for bringing together people who are going through similar struggles in order to help them find relief and comfort. There are groups for people who have lost children and spouses, for those who are fighting addictions and sicknesses, for those who want to overcome anger or fears. Today, support groups are available for just about anything you can think of. People find a greater understanding of what they are going through if they attend one of these meetings. Well, Jesus is "a man of sorrows and acquainted with grief" (Isa. 53:3, *NASB*). He understands all the groups! In fact, He understands you better than you understand yourself. When you join His group, you are embarking on an eternal communion with the One who understands you more than anyone or anything else.

A God Thought

God is crying out to you:

> My child, I understand you better then you understand yourself. I know the real you! I know the you that has yet to fully blossom in many ways and has felt so misunderstood and written off time and time again. I know what has been behind every win and every loss in your life. I know all of your secret

dreams and aspirations and all of your most terrifying fears and hurts. I am your support group. I am available now and always to be your wisest counselor, sympathetic group member and closest friend!

Note

1. Philip P. Bliss, "Hallelujah, What a Savior!"

CHAPTER SIX

HE COMFORTS ME

Blessed are they that mourn: for they shall be comforted.
MATTHEW 5:4, *KJV*

*Praise be to the God and Father of our Lord Jesus Christ,
the Father of compassion and the God of all comfort, who
comforts us in all our troubles, so that we can comfort those
in any trouble with the comfort we ourselves have received
from God. For just as the sufferings of Christ flow over into
our lives, so also through Christ our comfort overflows.*

2 CORINTHIANS 1:3-5

There was a four-year-old child whose next-door neighbor
was an elderly gentleman who had recently lost his wife.
Upon seeing the man cry, the little boy went into the old
gentleman's yard, climbed onto his lap and just sat there.
When his mother asked him what he had said to the neighbor,
the little boy said, "Nothing. I just helped him cry."

ANONYMOUS

**Many of us, like the people whose stories we've read
in this book, have experienced a comfort and peace
that we couldn't explain while enduring the most
traumatic of circumstances.** That's because the God
we worship isn't just the God of truths, facts and
numbers; He is also the God of compassion, kindness
and comfort. In fact He calls Himself the wonderful
counselor and Prince of Peace (see Isa. 9:6).

This earthly Christian life can seem to be a never-
ending struggle of running to the crumbling comforts of this world and then back to the rock-solid,
never-ending comfort of our eternal God. I'll never
forget waking up to a raging earthquake in 1994.
I was living in Hollywood, California, going to music
school, when I was suddenly wakened by a shaking
bed and the sight of what looked like paper-thin walls
twisting and buckling. It was like I was on a wild ride at

Disneyland. When the earthquake stopped, I heard people screaming and car alarms going off. (I heard those things every day, living in my apartment in Hollywood, by the way!) But the strange thing was, I felt an unexplainable peace within me through the whole ordeal. I thought to myself, the Prince of Peace is with me today. I have had several experiences in my life like this, and I thank God for them; but it's usually the day-to-day trials and worries that can be the hardest to shake off. I am forever learning how to run toward and get under the shadow of His wing. For me the way I find my way back to Him is through worship. When I begin to worship God in the midst of heartache or circumstances I don't understand, my perspective changes. Basically, this is how I am able to fix my eyes on Jesus, who is the author and perfecter of my faith (see Heb. 12:2).

Troubled Heart
By Mike Kalapp

My wife and I traveled to Florida for a vacation in March 2002. When we arrived at our condo on the west coast of Florida, I began to unload our luggage.

Immediately I experienced the classic symptoms of a heart attack. My father had died of a heart attack at age 62, so I knew the symptoms. I had all of them!

We were strangers to the area, but God led us to just the right hospital. I was quickly admitted to the emergency room and was immediately seen by a cardiologist. It was determined that I was having a heart attack. The next morning, a team of cardiologists told me that I would need to have an angiogram. This would be the best way to determine the extent of my heart disease.

That night, after my wife went back to the condo we were staying in, I entered the battle of my life, spiritually speaking. I was alone in the room and paced like a caged tiger from about 11:00 P.M. to around 2:30 A.M. It felt like all of the demons of doubt and fear had come to my room. How could I, the man who had been saved since age 17, who had pastored a church and prayed for so many fearful and doubting people, be so afraid? How could I, who preached so many messages on faith, be so faithless? How could I, who saw God be God so many times, doubt Him so? To be honest, I was ashamed of myself, but I couldn't seem to get on top of it.

Around 2:30 A.M., totally exhausted, I cried out to God: "God I need to know that You are here for me—right now. Not just in the past, but right now! I am going to look at Your Word for help. But before I do that, I am going to worship You with the CD I have." (One of my staff had handed me a CD of worship songs on my way out of town.) I sat down in the chair in my totally dark hospital room and turned the player on. The words I heard went like this:

I have a maker
He formed my heart
Before even time began
My life was in His hands

He knows my name
He knows my every thought
He sees each tear that falls
And hears me when I call

I began to weep uncontrollably in worship and gratitude to a loving God who spoke to me, while so afraid and faithless, in such a tender way. Even now my eyes are filled with tears, remembering His tender touch! I continued to listen:

I have a Father
He calls me His own
He'll never leave me
No matter where I go

He knows my name
He knows my every thought
He sees each tear that falls
And hears me when I call

As I continued to weep uncontrollably and worship the Lord, a peace came over me that I cannot explain. It really was a peace that surpasses all understanding (see Phil. 4:7). When I turned on the light so that I could read from the Psalms, I discovered that "He Knows My Name" was actually track five of the CD. How did the CD skip to track five? I know! God wanted me to hear the words I needed most right then. I have a maker who formed my heart, and even before time began, my life was in His hands! After some time in the Word, I fell sound asleep and had to be awakened the next morning.

The angiogram revealed nine major blockages. By God's grace, I was able to return to Los Angeles for surgery. I had five bypasses to repair all the blockages. God comforted me in my trial, and today I am in perfect health and God is blessing my life in so many ways.

I recently sang at the funeral of my cousin, Kim Sanders Walker. She was about my age and had two young children of her own. Though our family prayed and prayed, she was never healed. To this day, I don't understand why God heals some and doesn't heal others. But one thing I do know: He's always available to bring comfort! Jesus gave His followers the promise that the Comforter—the Holy Spirit—would be with us forever (see John 14:16, *KJV*).

> **JESUS IS RELEASING AND ENCOURAGING US TO BE JOYFUL EVEN WHEN WE FIND OURSELVES IN THE MIDST OF LIFE'S CHALLENGES, STRUGGLES AND TRAGEDIES.**

How people roll up their sleeves and try to endure such tragedies by their own strength is something I'll never know. Psalm 46:1 says that He is available to be our "ever-present help in [times of] trouble." Jesus did in fact tell us that "in the world ye shall have tribulation," but He went on with the promise, saying we could "be of good cheer, I have overcome the world" (John 16:33, *KJV*).

Though we may not totally grasp the depth of meaning of this verse, we do know a couple of things that Jesus is definitely saying here. First, I think Jesus is releasing and encouraging us to be joyful even when we find ourselves in the midst of life's challenges, struggles and tragedies. During these times, we can still, by His grace and indwelling Holy Spirit, be cheerful—even to the point of rejoicing! This is an important way we can express our faith, and it also helps defeat the strategies of our enemy (the devil), our weak flesh and the pull toward discouragement and fear.

Certainly there are times to mourn. Jesus not only acknowledges those times when He says, "Blessed are they that mourn" (Matt. 5:4, *KJV*), but He also instructs us to empathize with others—to "mourn with those who mourn" (Rom. 12:15). In this way, we comfort others as we ourselves have been comforted.

At the deepest level, we can always be of good cheer and experience the comfort of the Holy Spirit in our lives. Why, and how? Not because of the circumstances of the moment, and not because we look around at the evil and suffering that is all around us in this world, but because He has overcome it all!

Much of our lives seem to be in process from the perspective of our limited time frame. In other words, it doesn't feel like we're overcoming. However, if you read the end of the Bible, it says that we win! Good triumphs over evil! Jesus puts all of His enemies under His feet, and He reigns in victory and glory forever and ever (see 1 Cor. 15:24-25; Rev. 11:15)! Hebrews 2:8-9 says, "Yet at present we do not see everything subject to him. But we see Jesus, who was made a little lower than the angels, now crowned with glory and honor."

The second thing Jesus is saying here is that we will live in eternity and that our earthly life is not the end of the story. In fact, life on Earth is just a blip on a radar screen—less than a microsecond of time in our true lifespan—because our true lifespan is eternal if we have accepted and taken hold of God's incredibly generous offer of salvation through Jesus Christ. When we take this eternal perspective, we also find great comfort—comfort because we know that our God will make things right on that great day when Jesus returns and reigns in the new heaven and new earth. Our comfort is further secured in knowing that He removes all our sorrows, heals all our wounds and wipes away all our tears.

Sometimes the greatest comfort comes in knowing that this world is not our home. Jesus will come for us one day. Like the verse says, "Amen. Come, Lord Jesus" (Rev. 22:20).

A God Thought

Now we see but a poor reflection as in a mirror; then we shall see face to face. Now I know in part; then I shall know fully, even as I am fully known.

1 Corinthians 13:12

I'm the God who knows how to turn your mourning into dancing and your fear into joy! Where you see hopelessness, I see hope; where you see loss, I see gain. Your endings are My beginnings, and your final earthly breath will be turned into your first eternal shout! The people and circumstances of your life offer many words; but never forget that My word will be the last word! And My word says that you will dwell with Me forever and ever in My everlasting love!

Do not fear, for I am with you; do not be dismayed, for I am your God. I will strengthen you and help you; I will uphold you with my righteous right hand.

Isaiah 41:10

CHAPTER SEVEN

HE LISTENS TO ME

Anyone who comes to me, I will never turn away.
JOHN 6:37

[You] will call upon me, and I will answer [you]; . . .
I will deliver [you] and honor [you] . . .
and show [you] my salvation.
PSALM 91:15

Children can say the funniest things that are also so profound. More and more I'm learning how to listen to what God many times is saying through them when they speak.

You can pick up on this little boy's unquestioned confidence that God hears his prayers: "Dear God, thank You for the baby brother, but I think You got confused, because what I prayed for was a puppy."

Or how about this little girl's prayer: "Dear God, I didn't think orange went with purple until I saw the sunset You made on Tuesday. That was cool."

Something funny my two-year-old daughter, Eileen, does from time to time when she's hurt or displeased and begins to cry is that she not only cries, but she also *tells* us she's crying. In the midst of shrieks and moans, she shouts and declares, "Mommy, I'm crying!" In other words, "Are you listening? Do you hear me? Do you understand what's going on here? Stop the world; I have a problem here!"

How many times have you prayed and felt like your prayer never made it past the ceiling of your room? You felt like shouting, "God, hello! I'm here, do you hear me? Hello, God, anybody home?"

The Bible assures us that He does hear us: "His ears are open to their prayers" (1 Pet. 3:12, *NKJV*).

I don't know about you, but to know that the God of the universe is listening to me means everything. Even when He doesn't answer my prayer in the way I want it answered, I know that I have been heard, and I can trust that He'll do what is best!

He Heard My Cry
By Pastor Tim White

Dale Loos and his family attend the church at which I serve as pastor, Trinity United Church of Christ in Quincy, Illinois. Dale is 44 years old, married to Jeanna, the director of Christian Education at our church, and is a lieutenant in the Quincy Fire Department. Dale and Jeanna are blessed with two beautiful children, Eric and Erin.

Because of irregular blood work, Dale had a bone-marrow biopsy in May 2003. The test was to rule out leukemia. (Dale's father died after a brief battle with leukemia when Dale was eight years old.) On June 2, 2003, Dale was diagnosed with acute leukemia. The diagnosis terrified Dale and Jeanna, particularly in light of Dale's family history. Dale was told that a bone-marrow transplant or a T-cell transplant probably would be in his future.

Dale and Jeanna were devastated and thought of calling me to come to their home and pray with them. Instead they made the decision to show up at church near the end of our praise band practice and ask the whole praise band to pray with them before they left for Saint Louis, Missouri, the next morning.

When Dale and Jeanna came into the sanctuary near the end of our rehearsal time, it was obvious they had been crying and that their world had been shattered. They walked up to me, and Dale fell into my arms, sobbing. Then they told me about the results of the bone-marrow biopsy and how they hoped the whole praise team would pray together for them.

I gathered the band together and shared Dale and Jeanna's devastating news and their prayer request. I went on to talk about the laying on of hands in the New Testament and explained how many times in the Bible the sick received the laying on of hands and were healed. I then asked them if they would lay hands on Dale and pray with me for the Holy Spirit to be poured out on this family and for Dale to be healed. Everyone agreed that we should do this. I asked our keyboard player to play "He Knows My Name" quietly while we prayed.

Now you should understand this is something that has *never* happened in our church before. Our church is a very formal church that can be uptight when it comes to praying, demonstrating devotion in worship and the working of the Holy Spirit.

We gathered near the altar, and with Dale in the center, we all laid hands on him as I began to pray. That night a surge of the Holy Spirit carried us all to a new place in our faith. There were tears in every eye, and the heartfelt intercession for God's healing presence had never been so powerful in this place. When I paused to take a breath, someone else started praying. When that person stopped praying, another voice led our pleas for God's divine intervention.

We prayed without stopping for what must have been 35 or 40 minutes. Eventually, I said, "Let's sing 'He Knows My Name' to Dale, to remind him that we stand on the promises of God's love when we pray." While all of us continued to lay hands on Dale and Jeanna, we tearfully and confidently sang.

To this day, I cannot hear that song without feeling the presence of the Holy Spirit, and I cannot sing it without crying. Dale received chemotherapy treatments for his leukemia and never needed a bone-marrow transplant. On Christmas Day 2003, Dale returned to work at the Quincy Fire Department with no restrictions and a cancer-free diagnosis!

God used this whole experience to change the lives of the people in our praise band. We now end rehearsals with an extended time of prayer. Periodically, people in the church call and say, "I know the praise band is practicing tonight, would you ask them to pray for me?"

One of the greatest ways to make someone feel valued is to listen to him or her. People who are good listeners will always have a lot of friends, because everyone wants to be heard. God shows us value by listening to us. The praise band of Trinity United Church of Christ showed Dale and Jeanna value by listening to them. Are you in a situation now in which you can listen to others? Most of us are.

For example, husbands, how many times has your wife poured out her heart to you and your knee-jerk reaction is to cut the story short so that you can jump in and fix it (or fix her)? Then, of course, you are dumbfounded when she doesn't appreciate your logic and your quick fix. You are even more perplexed when she clams up altogether. Most of the time, our wives just want to be heard. Of course, this is just an example, the roles can be reversed, and this illustration can also apply to any close relationship. The truth is, we all want to be heard. Many times the greatest kindness and consideration we can receive is to have someone listen to us.

TELL HIM YOUR WINS; TELL HIM YOUR LOSSES. TELL HIM YOUR JOY; TELL HIM YOUR PAIN. HE IS LISTENING!

Isn't it amazing to think that our Father God wants to hear every detail of our hearts? This may be hard to believe, but it's true that the One who rules the universe is interested in everything about you— the good, the bad and the ugly.

Did you know that the Psalms are filled with laments, or complaints? The Bible considers prayers of lament to be worship! The reason for this is because the God of the Bible is the only God who cares about the pain, suffering and details of our lives. While He's altogether magnificent and mighty, He's also overwhelmingly loving and tender toward us.

Tell Him your wins; tell Him your losses. Tell Him your joy; tell Him your pain. He is listening! The Bible says to "pray without ceasing" (1 Thess. 5:17, *NASB*). This means a constant, all-day conversation with the Almighty. Tell Him all about your gratitude, your complaints, your concerns, your requests. This is part of your worship. In fact, to "pray without ceasing" is actually rather childlike when you think about it. It is keeping yourself constantly open, vulnerable and transparent before God, which is what He desires from us. Just like children who keep their parents updated on everything going on in their lives, we should do the same with our Father God. Jesus said, "Whoever does not receive the kingdom of God like a child will not enter it" (Luke 18:17, *NASB*).

So when my daughter Eileen announces, "Mommy, I'm crying!" she is, in a way, modeling this pure child-like approach to the God who listens to us. I believe God is calling each and every one of us to that place of honest crying out where we can commune with the Almighty and wait for His reply. Scripture says, "Surely the arm of the LORD is not too short to save, nor His ear too dull to hear" (Isa. 59:1).

I received a note from Deanna Perata, in which she commented on the words of "He Knows My Name" and described how it makes her bow in humility and admiration toward a God who would take the time to know her and know her every thought. Deanna wrote, "When I sing the words, 'He sees each tear that falls, and hears me when I call,' I feel like I am in a cornfield somewhere where no one can see me. I can share my deepest sorrows and let my deepest needs out and only He can find me. He comes to share in all the things that concern me and never judges but, rather, bends down to kiss my face and wipe away the tears. He brings to me, in that place of quiet shelter, the confidence I need to trust Him in *all* things. His interest in me is altogether good, and I am helped by His tender mercies each time I come to Him, because He knows me and listens to me."

A God Thought

Greater love has no one than this, that he lay down his life for his friends.
JOHN 15:13

Take heart, my child, for I am the God who sees and hears! I heard your first cry the moment you were born, and I've been listening to you ever since. Your cries for help are as sweet to Me as your songs of praise. I haven't asked you to pray and cast your cares on Me to fulfill some sort of religious ritual. I have instructed you to do this to remind you that I care and that I am here. Just as you speak and listen to me, so I will speak and listen to you. This is what friends do, and I am the God who calls you friend.

CHAPTER EIGHT

HE "FATHERS" ME

It is your Father's good pleasure to give you the kingdom.
LUKE 12:32, *NKJV*

[God is] a father to the fatherless.
PSALM 68:5

Aren't you glad that God isn't just the creator God but also Father God? God as our heavenly Father is one of the central themes of the New Testament. Jesus took this theme to a new level when He spoke of God as *Abba*—an affectionate Aramaic word best translated as "Daddy." It is interesting that the Old Testament only refers directly to God as Father 18 times. These are wonderful passages, but the point is that the idea of God as our Father is only touched on in the context of the whole of the Old Testament writings. The intertestamental literature (Jewish writings during the time between the Old and New Testaments) only refers to God as Father 4 times. These references tie God's fatherhood to His kingship and to our obligation to obey Him. However, Jesus, in the New Testament, speaks of God as Father 146 times. The fact that Jesus understood this relationship, taught it by His language and related to God as Father on an unprecedented and intimately personal level is another of the many proofs of the authenticity of Jesus' teachings, His ministry and His personhood (He is God the Son).[1]

The fact that God is not only our maker but also our loving Father is so important, because while masters, kings and lords represent tribes and nations, fathers represent families!

A Daughter of the King
By Donna Phillips

As a 12-year-old girl, I found it hard to understand why my life was falling apart. My family and I had always done the "right" things. We were Christians and active members in a local church. My father was a Sunday School teacher, chairman of the deacons, chairman of the pulpit committee—you name it, he did it. During the week, my dad taught computer classes at the community college in our town. It was there that my life began its downward spiral.

It was a beautiful day in April when an irate student went over the edge to express his anger over a grade. He walked into my father's class after it had begun, pulled out a gun and aimed it at my father. Another student stepped in to try to help. The gunman shot the young hero, and then he shot my father. Both men died that day. Much of me died, too.

I was Daddy's little girl. I loved going to the "office" with him on Saturdays, taking nature walks with him and just sitting on his lap to "help" him grade papers. Little did I know that one of those papers belonged to a man who would steal so much from me.

I remember going to the cemetery one day and having a one-way conversation with my father that went something like this: "Why did you leave me, Daddy? I thought you loved me. No one seems to understand what I am going through. Oh, they pretend to understand, but how could they possibly know how bad it hurts? I feel so alone. I try to keep the memories alive, but they seem to be slipping away. You left so suddenly; I didn't even get to say good-bye. I can't find a way to fill the hole in my heart where you used to be. I need you, Daddy!

"Life at home is not the same without you. Sis has her boyfriend to love, and now Mom's dating. I have no one. School is really tough, too. I look around and hear people talk about their perfect lives, and I feel so cheated. When something good does happen at school, I can't wait to share it with you, but then it hits me that you aren't coming home. Even Pepper waits by the door for you to come home at night. Why did you have to go? It's just not fair. You never hurt anyone. Why did this have to happen to our family? Nobody knows me like you do. No one understands how much I miss our times together. I will never, ever again have a father. There's no one to pick me up, swing me around and call me one of your nicknames like 'toad frog' or 'princess.' I miss that so much. It made me feel like I was more special than anyone else. I guess I am nobody's princess now."

I'll never forget those feelings of pain, fear, loneliness, grief, anger, frustration and depression—too many feelings for one person to feel at one time. I remember thinking that I was the only one in the world who had ever lost someone to death. I had never felt so alone.

And then there was the anger. One day I closed myself in my bedroom and began to cry out to God, not to ask for His help, but to blame Him. I threw things and hit the wall—you know, anger at its best.

Then my anger began to turn to bitterness. At church they preach forgiveness; but forgiveness for a murderer? In my eyes, a worthless man took the life of a great man. Is there really any room for forgiveness there?

Yet God says there is plenty of room for forgiveness. It is the forgiveness that Jesus asked from the Father for us as He hung on the cross (see Luke 23:34). His forgiveness extended to His murderers, and it extends to me. This is what eventually taught me to forgive. I finally began to pray, "Father, forgive him."

Even after I began to forgive, I still dealt with loneliness. Yet as I began to turn to God, He began to comfort me. In my loneliest hours, He was there with His arms around me, replacing the arms of my earthly father. God began to heal me with His love and His promises.

When I ached over the loss of my earthly father, my heavenly Father promised that He would be a father to the fatherless. He never took His eyes off me; He never missed a tear. I *do* have a Father, and He created me to be His own. He has never left me. He's my Father; He's my Abba—my Daddy. It brings me such comfort and security to know that He knows my name. He always knew my name, because I am His child—a child of the King, a true princess.

God invented the family to illustrate the closest bonds of intimate relationship we humans can ever know. I think it's for this reason that the enemy, through the ages, has worked overtime to destroy families. And it appears that he especially targets the relationship between earthly fathers and their children.

A Father to the Fatherless
By Danny Cross

My parents divorced when I was 4. Between the ages of 5 and 15, I saw my father a total of eight times, usually for 5 days. I saw him once when I was 27, and a final time when I was 29. As much as I wanted and needed a father, he chose not to be there.

I cried like a baby at his funeral in 1994, not because I would miss him so much, but because the finality that I would never have a father was too overwhelming.

Funny thing about my biological father, he never once came to see me (I always had to go see him). And he rarely said my name. The only time I can remember his saying my name was when he was manipulating me to see if I had any spending money for my visit. I would have given him all my spending money just to hear him call my name, just to hear him say, "I love you."

When I was 9 years old, my mom remarried. To this day I really don't understand why they married; they had little in common. But I lived in his house and I called him Daddy. He called me boy or Helen's boy (that's my mom). I had a dog named Ladd that he called son. He would sit with my dog on the porch and put his arm around Ladd's neck and talk to him about his day and call him son. He never called me son; and from 1968, when I first met him, until 1992, when he passed away, he never once, not even once, said my name. As a child, I would have given anything to hear him call my name. By the time I was a teen, I was so disillusioned with our relationship that I just avoided him, just as he avoided me. Sometimes we would go six months living in the same house without seeing each other.

To this very day, I have a difficult time maintaining close friendships with men. Because there were no men there for me when I was young, I suppose I carried that expectation into my adult life. I struggle daily with feelings of inadequacies about my own abilities as a father. I have known this whole lack-of-a-father thing was a sore point in my life, but I have never had it become as real and focused as it has become during this last year or so.

A while back a friend introduced me to a song that tore my heart open and made me face the pain as I had never faced it before. And yet, when the song broke me, and the tears flowed, and I sobbed out loud, wanting to cry out, "Please tell me you love me,

Daddy!" suddenly, I felt as if the Holy Spirit put His arms around me. I began to sing and weep, but this time for the joy of realizing that "I have a Father—He calls me His own; He'll never leave me no matter where I go. He knows my name. He knows my every thought. He sees each tear that falls, and He hears me when I call."

Isn't it interesting how it's the fathers who usually disappear in this world? On average, men live fewer years on Earth than do women. It's the fathers who many times do not seem to communicate the love and affection their kids so desperately need. It is from the fathers that children long to hear words of validation and affirmation. And I can't begin to count how many stories I've heard in which children feel that no matter what they do it isn't quite good enough.

There is no doubt about it, these are the forces of hell working overtime to try and distort our concept and understanding of our heavenly Father. I'm so glad the Bible speaks prophetically about how in the last days God will "turn the hearts of the fathers to their children, and the hearts of the children to their fathers" (Mal. 4:6).

In my devotions the other day, I sensed the Lord telling me to let Him father me. I thought to myself, *How do I let God be my Father—He being the perfect, holy, loving Father?* Then these words came to me:

1. *Fathers love to teach.* As a dad, I can tell you that if you ever want to make your dad's day, ask him something he knows a lot about and act real interested. Let your heavenly Father, through the Bible, teach you His unparalleled words of wisdom.

2. *Fathers love to witness their kids enjoy and love each other.* Think about the incredible, historical Christian family members you have: the patriarchs of the Old Testament, the apostles of the New Testament, the martyrs and Church reformers down through the ages. The Bible refers to these people as your family members who surround you as "a great cloud of witnesses" (Heb. 12:1). Can you believe it? Those people are your brothers and sisters. Tell God how grateful you are that you get to be a part of such an incredible band; then call a fellow Christian and just love and affirm

that person today. This definitely brings a smile to the heart of God!

3. *Fathers (normal, happy, healthy fathers, that is) love to affirm their kids, because nothing makes them happier than to see their kids meet their full potential.* Let God affirm you today. Listen to this: You can do all things through Christ who strengthens you (see Phil. 4:13); and "he will rejoice over you with singing" (Zeph. 3:17).

4. *Fathers love to receive affirmation from their children.* When you give your father honor and respect, making him feel like you truly love being associated with him, you affirm him. For me, this means worship! I like pastor and author John Piper's spin on the Westminster Confession: "Worship God by enjoying Him forever!"

God calls Himself our Father because He wants us to have an ongoing intimate relationship with Him. The older I get, the clearer it becomes. The most important things in our lives are our relationships. First, our relationship with God and then our relationships with people.

Every time I attend a funeral, I am reminded of one thing. It didn't matter what things the person had acquired; it mattered who he or she knew and who knew them! This is why it cuts to the deepest

> **THE MOST IMPORTANT THINGS IN OUR LIVES ARE OUR RELATIONSHIPS. FIRST, OUR RELATIONSHIP WITH GOD AND THEN OUR RELATIONSHIPS WITH PEOPLE.**

part of our being when we hear the words "I have a Father; He calls me His own." God is giving us the most important and precious thing we all long for— *relationship*—that deep, authentic, loving, soul-satisfying connection with Him that makes us complete!

A GOD THOUGHT

In addition to being the majestic, holy and glorious God of all, He is, indeed, our Daddy. We never have to wonder what He thinks of us, because He tells us in so many different ways. This next story, by Beth Mader, poignantly illustrates how God demonstrated to her that she was His very own.

In early 2001, I was in the midst of my wedding preparations. At the same time, my 72-year-old father was in the end stages of Alzheimer's disease. The heartbreaking reality of his decline meant it was unlikely that he would be able to walk me down the aisle on my wedding day.

One day, as I struggled with choosing who could take my dad's place in that important moment, I listened to a worship tape a friend had sent to me. When the worship team sang "He Knows My Name," it hit me: *Even though my biological father doesn't know my name anymore, my heavenly Father always will.*

In that moment, it became clear that my walk down the aisle wouldn't be without my dad; it would be with Jesus. I couldn't think of a more fitting tribute to my dad, and to Jesus, than to walk down the aisle to the song "He Knows My Name." It was a bittersweet yet beautiful moment. Thank you, Tommy, for writing the song. And thank you, Jesus, for walking me down the aisle.

Note

1. The information in this paragraph was based on the work of Joachim Jeremias, *The Central Message of the New Testament* (Philadelphia: Fortress Press, 1965).

CHAPTER NINE

HE WANTS ME

*For the LORD takes delight in his people; he crowns
the humble with salvation.*

PSALM 149:4

*Come to me, all you who are weary and burdened,
and I will give you rest. Take my yoke upon you and learn
from me, for I am gentle and humble in heart, and you
will find rest for your souls. For my yoke is
easy and my burden is light.*

MATTHEW 11:28-30

*For God so loved the world that he gave his one
and only Son, that whoever believes in him shall not
perish but have eternal life.*

JOHN 3:16

Something I've heard adoptive parents say to their child is "You're special because we got to pick you." The Bible uses the same language to talk about how much God wants us to be His own. It talks about being His adopted children and goes on to say that because God takes this "adoption" so seriously, He has made us "joint heirs with Christ" (Rom. 8:15,17, *NKJV*). We're full-on members of God's family and share in the whole inheritance!

God took it to the limit to secure our adoption and demonstrate His genuine, oh-so-personal bear hug kind of love for us. How did He do that? He sent Jesus, His only begotten Son, to lay down His life for us by way of a torturous death on a cross. In that act, He showed us and proved to us—in the most earthy, real way—just how much He truly wants us.

Precious in His Sight
By Thais Doyle

In February 1999, my husband and I received a call that a baby had been born to a cocaine-addicted mother and had been abandoned in a local hospital. The baby was now eight months old and had been living in foster care for most of her short life. Could we come see her? Would we consider adopting her? This was quite unexpected news, because we had tried for many years to adopt a child but had given up. We had not pursued any form of adoption for at least three years prior to this call. We had two older boys in school, and I was working full-time as a worship minister at a church. Our lives were very full. We weren't sure what God was doing in our lives at this point—the timing seemed all off—but we couldn't ignore God's leading.

We visited this little baby in her foster home a few days later and learned through our social worker that she had never been given a name. The social services agency discouraged the foster family from giving her a name that might be changed later by an adoptive family, so they had been calling her "baby girl." As I held this sweet baby for the first time—a beautiful little girl with big brown eyes and curly brown hair—it troubled me greatly that we had no name for her.

Our decision was not difficult. We knew that we would bring her home. The agency gave us only two days to make preparations. The first thing I did was to get out several baby-name books. I would *not* bring home this baby without a name. She would no longer be a throwaway baby, an abandoned baby, or a "drug baby." To us, she was very much wanted, very much longed for, very much loved.

We also made all of the other normal preparations of expectant parents. We bought a car seat and shopped for all of the essentials. But the question still loomed: What would we name her? I pored through baby-name books. We had family discussions and we talked with relatives on the phone.

Right around the same time, I began working with one of our worship teams on a new Tommy Walker song. In fact, we had started learning "He Knows My Name" a few weeks before the phone call about our baby. I had liked the song; but as I now searched through baby-name books, I couldn't shake the tune from my head—and these particular words from the song, which seemed to be written specifically for my new little one:

> I have a Father
> He calls me His own
> He'll never leave me
> No matter where I go

What incredible comfort and reassurance for someone who had been abandoned!

We brought Breanne Elizabeth Doyle home on February 27. Today Breanne is five-and-a-half years old. She has been a part of our family for just under five years. She is such a joy and a blessing. Words will never describe the love that we have for this little daughter that God gave us. Breanne knows the song "He Knows My Name." It has been sung to her many times. Though she is still too young to comprehend the magnitude of its message, we want her to know that we serve a God who knows her and loves her, and He even knew her name before we did!

On my last trip to the Philippines, in 2003, I met two young brothers, Bitoy and Agong Montenegro. Alex Chua, their pastor, told me their amazing story.

The parents of these boys were a father who was an irresponsible drunkard and a mother who was a battered wife and who left the family when the boys were young. The boys were never able to locate her whereabouts.

Bitoy and Agong were only seven and five years old when they were put in a sack by their father and thrown into the ocean. A neighbor rescued them from drowning. Their father was put in prison for a couple of months but was later released because the boys' grandmother took pity on him.

Because of this horrible situation and because nobody wanted them, the two brothers were forced to live on the streets. This is where they learned to sniff glue, because it helps to take away hunger pains, and to steal in order to survive. The two brothers were very familiar with the police officers in the Agdao district. They had been in and out of jail more than 50 times. According to the boys, the only time they had a chance to take a bath was in jail.

In April 2001, God changed their lives. Now, Agong is a music leader in the church Alex Chua pastors, and he is helping other street children to learn musical skills, to worship and to be involved in the church community. As Pastor Chua told me, "God has transformed both brothers spiritually and personally. Now they have a future and a hope."

My friend, God not only knows you but He also wants you! Do you remember when you were a kid and it came time to pick teams and you desperately hoped you wouldn't be the last one picked? You knew that if you were picked last, you were only on the team by default. You felt unwanted. You felt like a leftover.

Too often we slip into thinking that maybe God only loves us by default—that somehow He set things up long ago by making a covenant to love everybody. Therefore, He has to love us, along with everybody else. To believe He truly wants us in a deliberate fashion—picking us for His team because we're special to

TO BELIEVE GOD TRULY WANTS US IN A DELIBERATE FASHION—PICKING US FOR HIS TEAM BECAUSE WE'RE SPECIAL TO HIM—IS A TRUTH THAT CAN ESCAPE US.

Him—is a truth that can escape us. But the high-impact message of the gospel is that your heavenly Father loves you so much that He wants you in His family so that you and He can enjoy one another's company for all eternity. If you can just grab that wonderful truth and run with it, you will know that you are affirmed and accepted.

Go ahead, accept it right now, in this moment. You have definitely been picked. Yes, you! In fact, the Bible tells us that God has chosen us in the Beloved (see Eph. 1:6). Revisiting the picking-of-teams analogy, some of you still haven't shown up for the game because you can't believe you've been invited to play. Maybe it's because you are having trouble overcoming rejection and hurt from your past; maybe your self-esteem is shattered. Perhaps you were abandoned like baby Breanne. Cry out to God and say, "Lord, help my unbelief! You said that 'the one who comes to Me I will by no means cast out'" (John 6:37, *NKJV*).

Maybe you can't show up for the game because you're having trouble believing that God really can and will forgive you for some particular sin. Cry out to God and say, "I can't stir up the feeling of being forgiven. Help me, Lord, to stand on Your promise that 'if we confess our sins, He is faithful and just to forgive us our sins and to cleanse us from all unrighteousness'" (1 John 1:9, *NKJV*). Nothing falls outside the scope of God's forgiveness.

Others of you still haven't shown up for the game because you need to wake up and smell the coffee and realize that the forces of darkness (Satan and his minions), people under the influence of evil and the distortions in our natural world do exist. Evil is at work to shape your thinking, your heart and your behavior in the wrong direction, which is in the opposite direction of God's love. Cry out to God and say, "Oh, Father, if you really do want me, here I am, just as I am, 'because greater is he that is in [me], than he that is in the world' (1 John 4:4, *KJV*). Speak the word, Lord, and I will be set free from these patterns of thinking and behaviors that threaten to destroy me."

Now is the time to overcome; the tip-off is here. God loves you and wants you. He desires you to be a part of His family for eternity. Check into the game and go for it! He won't disappoint you.

A GOD THOUGHT

God can't seem to say Acts 17:24-27 loud enough. Here is my paraphrase of those verses:

I want you! Why do you think I planned you, made you and then sent My Son to save you? In fact, I created the whole earth and set you in this particular time in history so that you would reach out to Me and find Me. I am not far from you!

CHAPTER TEN

HE'LL NEVER LEAVE ME

I will never leave you nor forsake you.

HEBREWS 13:5, *NKJV*

If I rise on the wings of the dawn, if I settle on the far side of the sea, even there your hand will guide me, your right hand will hold me fast.

PSALM 139:9-10

When I was a kid, for some reason I had a huge fear of being abandoned. I remember walking home from school every day in the fourth grade and peering around the corner to see if my mom's car was in the driveway.

I come from a big family, and I don't know why, but I just knew they were planning to leave me someday. My parents gave me no reason to feel this way, but I guess we always fear the very worst thing we could ever imagine. For me it was abandonment. A man named Eric also struggled with this fear but was delivered by the God who will never leave us.

Claimed by God
By Pastor Dale Walker

Eric was a worship leader at our church. He loved to lead the song "He Knows My Name," though he could almost never get through the song without tears flowing from his eyes.

Eric had been abandoned as a young boy and grew up in a children's home. As much as he tried to feel good about himself, he always felt like something was missing. He knew that he was a Christian and that God loved him, but in the revelation that came to him in the singing of that simple song, he finally and fully understood who he really is in Christ and knew that he always had been in the heavenly Father's arms.

The insecurities and feelings of abandonment evaporated in the knowledge of who He is to the God who loves and claims him as His son from all eternity past.

Sadly, many children have been abandoned in this world we live in. There are approximately 30,000 foster children in Los Angeles County alone.[1] I can hardly bear to think about the millions of street children in Third World countries. Have you ever had the opportunity to come alongside someone in need and offer your commitment and support? Belonging is not reserved for the few; people from all walks of life and all kinds of circumstances need connection and intimacy.

It is especially beautiful to see how the Holy Spirit can cause a characteristic intrinsic to God's nature to be formed in a person and cause others to be influenced by that life. This was Glen Vanlandingham's experience.

Uncompromising Commitment
By Glen Vanlandingham

Shortly after my father, who had been diagnosed with cancer, entered the hospital, he lost the ability and the will to communicate. But I had a lot of time to talk to him and thank him for being such a caring father who was always there for me. Even when times were tough, he made sure to set the right example.

One of the greatest ways he modeled character and commitment to me was when my mother was sick, also with cancer. He would take her to doctors' appointments and just sit with her and comfort her. His employer began to complain that Dad was spending too much time taking care of my mother. My dad quit on the spot, with nowhere else to go. As it happened, he was hired the next day for a higher paying job by a man who said that Dad could spend as much time with my mother as he needed.

When I hear Tommy's song, the phrase "He'll never leave me" reminds me of my dad's uncompromising commitment to support my mom in her time of weakness, to comfort her and not to leave her side.

Jesse
By Linda Walker

"Your deepest sorrow shall become your greatest joy." My mother-in-law spoke those words years ago, during a family prayer meeting held on behalf of our newborn son, Jesse, who had suffered a brain injury at birth.

Today my deepest sorrow concerning Jesse, who is now age 23 and suffering from severe cerebral palsy, is not all due to watching the physical hardship he has endured; I have also been dismayed at how very, very alone he is. He has a few people in his life who give him a little attention from time to time, but he spends the majority of his hours and days, though supervised, being alone. He always has.

Jesse has no friends, no one his own age to laugh or joke with. He has no girlfriends. Apart from a tremendous miracle, he will never be married and raise a family of his own. My son will never go to college, pursue a career or have a life he can call his own. On a lesser scale, he has never munched popcorn, bit into a juicy steak, licked ice cream or munched an apple. He's never sung a song or blown out birthday candles. He has never worn out the knees of his pants or the soles of his shoes. They are sadly intact when I put them in the giveaway bag because he's outgrown them. Jesse has never played a game, ridden a bike or tossed a football. He has also never read a single sentence or uttered a solitary word. Due to the spasticity that is part of cerebral palsy, a crippling condition due to loss of brain cells caused by lack of oxygen to the brain at birth, Jesse can probably kick a hole through a glass window or support a heavy weight on his upraised arms, but he can't scratch an itch or even protect himself from the smallest physical harm.

Jesse is what is termed "wheelchair bound." He has little to no head and trunk control and no purposeful movements of his arms and legs. One of Jesse's fellow sufferers, Christopher Nolan, refers to his condition, in his book *Under the Eye of the Clock* (written via computer with a head-pointer to strike the keys), as being "crucified to my bed."[2]

Jesse's enjoyments comprise simple sights taken in by his keen eyes and various sounds that catch his interest. He seems to enjoy the sights and sounds of a crackling fire, birds in the trees and everything from Bach to Dolly Parton, with contemporary Christian music in between. He recognizes faces, places and all kinds of phrases.

Sure, it's possible that some would think that perhaps Jesse is better off in some ways than the rest of us. Think of all the hassles of this trouble-filled, complex, sinful life he doesn't have to deal with! If one believes in heaven, as I do, it is easy to think that Jesse might have gotten some kind of free ticket through life and needs only to wait for the wonderful life ahead of him on the other side. That may be true. But between the reality he lives now and what is to come is an awfully long, lonely wait.

Sometimes, for no apparent reason, Jesse gets sad for a day, maybe two, and we find his eyes constantly welling up with tears while he attempts to vocalize something to us. We check and double check all his comfort needs until it becomes clear to us that he is simply expressing emotion.

As his mother, and speaking for his father, we are limited and can do just so much to enhance his world. It is very hard being the arms and legs for another human being. There is so much involved in just the everyday basic care of his bodily needs that there is little time left over for living life outside of these things.

We actually had a few doctors in the early years who implied that Jesse was not worth our time and trouble because of the inevitable loss of his lack of functional abilities. And when it comes to some acquaintances and friends, I have often thought if only I had a nickel for every time one of them said to me, "If it were me, I couldn't do what you do." I often feel like I am either a saint or a fool in their eyes; never what I really am—just a mother of a crippled child. How could I explain to them that one smile from my crippled son is worth more to me than a thousand other delights?

Sometimes, in the quieter moments, when the feeding pump has been tended, the medicines have been given, he's diapered and freshly clothed and is breathing comfortably, I pause and start to think about who Jesse really is. He isn't all those sad, difficult things that it takes to keep him alive and well. He isn't the silent, seemingly forgotten young man he appears to be. He is not the voiceless, futureless fellow we think he is. He's alone, perhaps lonely as well, but he is not forsaken.

As heart-wrenching as Jesse's predicament is, I have come to understand on a deeper level that there must be a reason and purpose to all of this. If a tiny sparrow cannot fall to the ground without our heavenly Father knowing about it, then I am certain He knows all about my son. If the hairs on our heads are numbered, knowing that we lose and gain some every day, there is no doubt that the Father knows about every choke, every gag, every prick of a needle, every cry and every lonely or fearful moment Jesse has ever had.

If this is so, then the creator and sustainer of the universe truly does know Jesse. The Lord knows him in a way that is well beyond what we can comprehend. This surety gives me tremendous hope and great comfort. *There is just something about knowing that God knows; that is all I need to know.*

My deepest sorrows have indeed become my greatest joy! The "peace that passes all understanding" has come. As my brother-in-law, Steve, says, "It is the peace you have when you really shouldn't be having it." All I know is that, though our son's care is getting harder, the load seems to get easier. His condition keeps worsening, but my fears keep subsiding. And though his earthly future looks bleaker, my expectations for the life to come only get brighter! I used to think I was living a nightmare that I could never wake up from. Now I have awakened to a reality that only God can impart to us because He knows us like He does.

What is the purpose of our struggles in this life? Isn't it to take us to the very edge of our own sufficiency so that God can overwhelm us with His grace, love, and mercy?

Half of a Miracle

Sorrow increases our capacity for joy,
Courage is born out of fear;
Peace is delivered by a raging tempest,
Victory through struggles and fears.

The negative is just the conduit
To bring the positive through;
Our need is one-half of a miracle.
The other half will come soon.

Perhaps your father abandoned you as a child. Or perhaps your father has passed away. Or perhaps your life or the life of someone who is close to you will never be lived within the boundaries of what one would call normal. Despite the losses we incur in life, we have a Father God who will absolutely never leave us, no matter where we go. I know that many of you are aware of this promise, but for those of you who have been abandoned or have had the fear of abandonment, this truth means everything. God with us is one of the Bible's major themes. God is not just somewhat near, but He is actually closer than the breath we breathe. God's Word says that He's behind us, before us, beside us, above us, below us and, best of all, living inside us (see Ps. 103:17; Isa. 52:12; 2 Tim. 4:17; Ps. 139:7-10; Col. 1:17,27).

Another beautiful verse says that He will "surround me with songs of deliverance" (Ps. 32:7). There have been times in my private devotions when I could almost physically sense God's presence surrounding me. It always has everything to do with simple faith and with being still long enough to finally be aware of His presence (see Ps. 46:10).

> **GOD IS NOT JUST SOMEWHAT NEAR, BUT HE IS ACTUALLY CLOSER THAN THE BREATH WE BREATHE.**

A more recent goal in my relationship with God is to learn how to recognize His voice. The first step is to be still and quiet. Have you ever wondered what life must have been like before cars, CD players and television sets? Recently, I saw people in Africa who walked for hundreds of miles with hardly a backpack on their back, let alone a carrying a portable audiocassette or CD player. Needless to say, they had a lot of time to think and, I hope, to pray. Even in the midst of my loud world, I have been sensing the nearness of God and hearing His still, small voice. As the old saying goes, If God feels far away, guess who left.

I hope that today you will be inspired to earnestly seek the manifest presence of God in your life, for He is in this very moment with you. He'll *never* leave you.

A GOD THOUGHT

It is in tragedy that I bring redeeming victory; it is in the thunder of the storm that you will hear Me say "Peace, be still." It is in the quiet of the night that My voice speaks your name. And it is when everyone else is gone that I will show you I am near.

Where can I go from your spirit? Where can I flee from your presence? If I go up to the heavens, you are there; if I make my bed in the depths, you are there. If I rise on the wings of the dawn, if I settle on the far side of the sea, even there your hand will guide me, your right hand will hold me fast. If I say, "Surely the darkness will hide me

and the light become night around me," even the darkness
will not be dark to you; the night will shine like the day,
for darkness is as light to you.
PSALM 139:7-12

Notes
1. "A Letter from the Executive Director," *The Alliance for Children's Rights.* http://www.kids-alliance.org/presidents_message.asp (accessed May 10, 2004).
2. Christopher Nolan, *Under the Eye of the Clock* (New York: St. Martin's Press, 1967), p. 130.

CHAPTER ELEVEN

HE'LL NEVER FORGET ME

Do not fear, for I am with you; do not be dismayed,
for I am your God. I will strengthen you and help you;
I will uphold you with my righteous right hand.

ISAIAH 41:10

Can a mother forget the baby at her breast and have
no compassion on the child she has borne? Though she
may forget, I will not forget you!

ISAIAH 49:15

Every one of us—despite our socioeconomic, cultural and ethnic backgrounds—is needy. When I say "needy," I am referring to our powerlessness without God, our weakness without Jesus Christ. The amazing thing is that God doesn't forget about us in our imperfection; rather, He runs to our side to lift us out of the muck and mire.

The following poem, based on Psalm 6, depicts how God will never forget us—the needy—nor will He forsake us. As so many passages of Scripture declare, one day God will set things right. Justice and righteousness shall reign in His Kingdom.

Good News! [Psalm 6]

The needs of the needy
Shall not be ignored forever.
The hopes of the poor
Shall not always be crushed.

The oppressed may come
To Him for justice,
He has never forsaken
The least ones who trust.

The first time I read the following story, I cried like a baby. You may or may not be known by people on this earth, but if the name of this book is true, and if only God knew your name, then you would be eternally and perfectly valued and known.

Nameless Graves
By JoAnn Butrin, Ph.D, R.N.

I've lived and worked in Africa for years and know that death, funerals and burial are very important to Africans. One day, in Zambia, on the way home from visitations to AIDS victims, a friend asked me if I would like to go by a cemetery. Already feeling very emotional over all that I had seen and heard that day, I wasn't sure if I was up to the cemetery, but suddenly we were in the middle of it.

Though I had heard about the unmarked graves, I had never actually walked among them before. Stretched as far as I could see were fresh mounds of dirt, most of which had not as much as a marker. Gravediggers worked around me, preparing for the 50 to 100 more people who would die in the next day or two. I doubt that anything could have prepared me for the sorrow I felt as I realized that no one knew who was buried in these graves. These people, in a sense, were forgotten. No one came to cry, to mourn or to leave flowers at the graves—a tragedy for anyone, but surely a tragedy for the Zambians who lay in these graves.

That evening as my friends and I gathered in one of their homes to cry and to pray and to try to process all that we had seen and heard, one friend played a soundtrack of the song "He Knows My Name." Suddenly, our talking ceased and we turned our attention to the words:

He knows my name
He knows my every thought
He sees each tear that falls
And hears me when I call

We all began to cry again, realizing that this was a message from the Lord Himself. True, no one on Earth knew who lay in those graves, but Jesus did. He knew every one by name. They were not unknown graves; they were known to the Father. He knew about the tears and the suffering and the fear of every person who had died.

Somehow the words of that song brought comfort and help to us. It also brought renewed inspiration to each of us to say that although AIDS is the worst medical emergency of our world, it is also the greatest evangelism opportunity. It made us want to be sure that everyone we came in contact with could know the name of Jesus and enter into eternity with peace, knowing that the Lamb Himself had recorded their names in the Lamb's book of life.

Once a year or so, I take a musical team and others to the poor and forgotten ones, a ministry we do here and around the world. We provide worship evangelism crusades, worship seminars and, for the poor, outreaches where we provide food and medicine. We call it giving our best to those who have the least. In other words, "Whatever you did for one of the least of these brothers of mine, you did for me" (Matt. 25:40).

In May 2003, a team from my church went to Zambia. On one of the first days of this particular trip, we traveled to a village outside of Ndola. It seemed as if we drove forever, got lost and drove some more. Finally, in the middle of nowhere, we drove up to a cinder-block building surrounded by traditional African grass huts. There were about 300 people waiting for us.

I thought, *Where did they come from? Where are we? Why are they all living here?* These were truly some of the forgotten people of the world. Hunger, malaria and AIDS were rampant. Most of the children didn't run and play but stood around with sad faces, waiting for food. One man told me that last year they ate only two or three meals a week. In recent months, because they ate one meal almost every day, he said they felt very blessed. In my travels, I have discovered that the children and adults who are literally starving to death do get some press, but there are millions upon millions who are barely surviving because of hunger almost every day of their lives. These are the forgotten ones, and when we remember them, we remember Him.

I'll never forget the sights and sounds of their worship. In the midst of their desperate need, they could always sing one more song to Jesus.

All this being said, you don't have to be a hungry African or an abused child to feel forgotten. You may be rich, poor, famous, average, married, single, young, old, successful, unsuccessful, shy or the life of the party. You may be surrounded every day with people—at work and at home—but still feel utterly isolated. At times, that happens to all of us.

It has been said that strong Christians are not strong people; it's just that they've learned where to run. They run to the truth: God thinks about them

IT'S BEEN SAID THAT STRONG CHRISTIANS ARE NOT STRONG PEOPLE; THEY HAVE JUST LEARNED WHERE TO RUN.

all the time, and they are not forgotten. They cling to the promise that if Jesus intercedes for them, they must be pretty important to Him. They let the great Comforter bring them comfort. And they continually find their significance in the most significant of all significant ones—God Himself!

Never Alone
By Tony Yeargin

For our Christmas Program in 2002, our band, orchestra and choir did "A Midnight Clear," a Praise Gathering concert that has a great version of "He Knows My Name" in it. My wife's father had died the

Thanksgiving before, and her mom was really feeling hopeless and lonely and was missing her husband tremendously. (They had been married 52 years, and he had accepted Christ just a few days before his death. So all of us were feeling bittersweet emotion.)

Sally and I had invited her mom to come to hear the music, hoping it would lift her spirits a bit. Sally was sitting beside her mom and told me afterwards that her mom had sobbed during "He knows My Name." It was a word from God to her mom that said she had not been forgotten and left to exist all alone—that He cared deeply for her and knew her by name.

When we experience difficult and hopeless times, the first thing the enemy wants to do is to make us feel isolated and alone. He wants to make us think that we're the only person on the planet who has ever experienced what we're experiencing and that no one else really cares. Essentially, the devil wants us to feel forgotten.

Not only has God *not* forgotten you, but also the Bible says He never stops thinking about you:

> How precious are your thoughts about me, O God! They are innumerable! I can't even count them; they outnumber the grains of sand! And when I wake up in the morning, you are still with me! (Ps. 139:17-18, *NLT*).

If constantly thinking about you isn't enough, He's praying for you, too.

> Christ Jesus, who died—more than that, who was raised to life—is at the right hand of God and is also interceding for us (Rom. 8:34).

Now that's an amazingly comforting thought. Jesus prays for and thinks about little ol' me and little ol' you.

A God Thought

Even though you forget about Me throughout your day, I never forget about you. Although your mind worries, falls into confusion, and many times thinks utterly self-absorbed thoughts, My thoughts are full of perfect wisdom and perpetual love for you. Don't forget, I'm not like you or any other who has ever lived before you. I'm the omnipresent, all-knowing Father of creation who has a perfect memory that is driven by My love and affection for you. I remember your first birthday and I'm never going to forget your last. Resist the lie that you are all alone in this world. You will never be forgotten, because you are Mine, and I do not forget!

CHAPTER TWELVE

HE'LL NEVER GIVE UP ON ME

I have loved thee with an everlasting love: therefore with lovingkindness have I drawn thee.

JEREMIAH 31:3, *KJV*

Praise the LORD, O my soul, and forget not all his benefits—who forgives all your sins and heals all your diseases. As far as the east is from the west, so far has he removed our transgressions from us.

PSALM 103:2-3,12

He who began a good work in you will carry it on to completion until the day of Christ Jesus.

PHILIPPIANS 1:6

From the moment of my conversion experience, I felt that God was telling me He had some special plans for me. No other words from the Lord have been more deeply moving to me yet more difficult to hold on to. It seems like no matter how much I accomplish, the first place the enemy goes with me is to tell me I'm worthless and I should give up. What a battle it has been!

GOD IS EVER SAYING, "TRY AGAIN!" HE'S THE GOD OF THE SECOND CHANCE!

I feel so passionate about this area of attack because I want everyone to be reminded that while the devil, difficult circumstances and sometimes the people who surround us can give us a lot of good reasons to throw in the towel, God is ever saying, "Try again!" He's the God of the second chance! Not only when it comes to conversion, but also when it comes to life's calling and purpose. Although, at times, we can be sinful, lazy and distracted, the good news is that God has already prepared a brand-new day for your tomorrow—a day with fresh new mercies (see

Lam. 3:23). He says He's for you, not against you (see Rom. 8:31), and He has predestined works specifically for you and you alone (see Eph. 2:10).

I have experienced times while leading worship at my church when I sensed that God was using me in the unique way for which He had predestined me. And I'll tell you what, there's nothing like it! There's nothing so life giving, energizing and joy-filled as living out God's calling in your life. I remember when I was at a large event at the Orange Bowl and watched hundreds of men give their lives to Christ while thousands of voices sang "He Knows My Name." It certainly didn't have anything to do with my being worthy of such an awesome sight and sound, but it had everything to do with God taking great delight in flowing through one of His children. Please know that the last thing I want to do is glorify myself or any kind of public ministry. The point here is that God had every right to give up on me years ago in the midst of my laziness, doubt, sin and everything else; instead, He took great joy in bringing to fruition those works He had planned for me to do. Some of you just need to be reminded that it's not over till it's over! God lives in and through His kids in millions of different ways; and by His grace He is ready, willing and waiting to start again with you today.

Message in a Bottle
By Peter Lim

My mind was racing faster than a racehorse, and I wondered if this was what was meant when people say your life flashes before your eyes just before you die. I tried to recall why I had gone to the overhead bridge. The sky had begun to drizzle—not heavily, but enough to add to my already heavy spirit.

The year was 1984. I had just entered junior college and was adjusting to a new school with new friends. I had been raised to be independent. My dad had passed away when I was nine years old, and Mum had been left to fend for her family of nine children. The journey had been difficult, to say the least. There was never enough money to provide for the family. At a very young age, several of my older siblings had to quit school and find work.

Our parents did not teach us how to get along with one another. We frequently fought and quarreled. John, the eldest, was the tyrant of the family. He ruled with an iron rod after Dad died. All of us hated him; but being the eldest son, he often got his way.

Tonight was no exception. John had, for the umpteenth time, left his cup unwashed in the sink. Mary, who never got along with him, made a remark. It was totally harmless and totally valid—Why couldn't he wash his own cup? Something so small erupted into a big fight. Angry words and expletives, as well as objects, flew through the air. Some of us younger ones ran to the kitchen to hide the knives. During one such fight, a chopping knife had been flung, which narrowly missed my mum.

When I was 17 years old and a junior college student, I decided that it was time to speak up. I shouted for the fighting to stop, but what a mistake that was. John, eager to start a new fight, turned his wrath on me. He verbally attacked my character and my faith in God and mocked me for being a "religious freak." Despite all that he said, I remember sensing an overwhelming peace within me. I was glad that someone like John had noticed God's presence in my life. And although he used it against me, I knew that I had lived my testimony well. Then, to everyone's shock, I laughed out loud. The joy of God had filled me in the midst of this heated exchange, and I saw the hot coals on his head turning blood red with angry fire.

"What's so funny?" John demanded, as he charged toward me while the rest of my siblings restrained him. I could not stop smiling, and I just shook my head as I walked out of the house.

It was then that my moment of weakness visited me. Memories of a childhood without Dad, the extremely soured relationships among my siblings, a very helpless mum caught in the middle—the tears welled up within me and flowed uncontrollably as I walked up the overhead bridge. After a while, I could not make out the difference between my tears and the rainy drizzle.

I tried so hard to grow up on my own. While blessed with sisters and good friends who loved me dearly, I felt so alone as I stood on that bridge. I looked down at the traffic below, dazzled by the bright head-lamps, and I remember hearing a very persuasive voice within me say "Jump!" As the voice grew louder, the anger and hatred of the earlier fight became very intense as I started to question God about the meaning of my life and whether I had lived long enough.

I now understand why people at the brink of sui-cide can be pushed beyond sanity to end their lives. Emotions overwhelm reason, and the easy way out seems to be to kill yourself. I was so close to making that mistake until God intervened. Out of nowhere, a group of men appeared just below the other end of the bridge, talking and laughing loudly as if they were drunk. They were not carrying umbrellas and they seemed to enjoy the rain. They stopped and looked up at me standing in the center of the bridge. "Jump down!" one of them shouted. "Jump down!" the rest echoed. They laughed loudly and walked on.

In an instant, I was awakened from my spiritual stupor! The human voices that asked me to jump to certain death, and which I believe to this day were meant to reinforce the devil's own voice within me, stopped me in my tracks.

Suddenly, I became very aware of what was about to happen. I pulled myself back from the railing to the middle of the bridge. I could almost hear the angels that surrounded me heave a sigh of relief. A smile returned to my face, and I shook my head in disbelief at what could have happened if I had listened to the voice in my head. To this day, I believe that God sent angels in the form of men to mock and ridicule me, knowing that by diverting my attention from my distorted thoughts I would listen more to my heart, where God's voice speaks!

Indeed, God knows my name and my every thought. I know that God collects every tear that has ever fallen from my eyes in a bottle, which He will present to me one day when I meet Him face-to-face. And I believe that with a smile, He will hand me those bottles and say to me, "Look, your tears have not been in vain. When you cried, you thought you were alone, but I was there to collect each tear that fell. No matter how many bottles I had to use, I didn't miss a drop!"

Peter heard two voices that day. He heard, "It's too late; it's too hopeless; just give up," and he heard the voice of our Savior: "It's never too late; my mercies are new every morning." Thank God that of the two voices, he chose to listen to the latter. One of the best ways to describe Jesus is to call Him our Redeemer. It is in His very nature to take what has been ruined, destroyed and even put to death and bring it back to health and life again.

I'll never forget when I wrote and taught the song "These Things Are True of You." One of my favorite lines in that song is "He never gives up on the hopeless ones." When I penned those words, I was thinking about how God doesn't give up on the dirty, homeless people; the addicts, the poor—you know all those "sinners" out there. I thought, *What a nice God, He doesn't give up on them.* Then a few days later, when I was teaching the song to my church, God turned the whole thing around on me. I heard Him say, "No, Tommy, you're the hopeless one." I began to weep uncontrollably in front of my whole church. I remembered all the ways I had failed God and sinned against Him in the past.

NOTHING WILL HELP YOU GET OUT OF BED EVERY MORNING LIKE KNOWING THAT GOD HAS SOMETHING SPECIAL FOR YOU THAT DAY, OR AT LEAST KNOWING THAT TODAY IS A BUILDING BLOCK TOWARD HIS AWESOME PLANS FOR TOMORROW.

There were many good reasons, in my mind, why God had every right to give up on me. I became so ashamed of my spiritual pride. God reminded me where I would be today if it weren't for His grace and His plan for my life.

In the life stories you have already read in this book, you have seen how God has time and time

again taken hopeless people and hopeless situations
and redeemed them into something good. While we
will never understand the whole picture, it is clear
that God has a plan—a calling and a purpose—for
everyone, and He is committed to this plan to the
very end (see Phil. 1:6).

Nothing will help you get out of bed every morning like knowing that God has something special for
you that day, or at least knowing that today is a building block toward His awesome plans for tomorrow.

There are a lot of hopeless and even suicidal people
in the world because they don't realize that in the
midst of every kind of disappointment and pain, God
is working. I completely understand that this is very
hard to understand at times, but the Bible says, "Where
there is no vision, the people perish" (Prov. 29:18, *KJV*).
It's interesting, because it's only the people "crazy"
enough to believe that God has something for them
who ever accomplish anything of lasting value.

I want to emphasize that God usually uses people
in ways that may not be considered public ministry.
I often think of stay-at-home moms like my mom and
my wife. My mother poured the love of Jesus into her
children in a profound way and now has watched
them bring thousands to Christ all over the world.

There are so many Christians, especially older ones, who have decided they have seen everything they are ever going to see when it comes to how God touches them and touches people through them. I believe this signals the beginning of the end of their spiritual walk and growth in Him. God is all about new beginnings, which is why He made years, months, weeks, days and, even within a day, morning, noon and night. If God hasn't given up on you, then why should you give up on you? Drink in His undeserved new mercies in this fresh new day and start again!

Do you truly believe in God's unconditional commitment to you? Do you truly believe He will never give up on you, even if you get lost in the deserts of life? I want to close with the story of a mother who lost her son. After reading it, I want you to multiply that mother's love times eternity. The result will be the Father's love for you!

Relentless Mother
Author unknown

One day, a little boy, much to the alarm of his mother, was missing from the village in which they lived. The town's people gathered and decided after searching the whole village that, unfortunately, the little fellow must have somehow wandered up into the very dangerous mountain that overlooked the village.

The problem was the mountain. It was a treacherous climb due to the severe cliff drops and precarious footholds. This caused the townspeople considerable doubt as to whether they could be successful in finding the boy.

But the mother of the lost child was completely frantic with fear and longing to have her boy found and back safely in her arms. So the townspeople decided to gather the strongest, most able-bodied men of the village to take on the search.

After many hazardous and unsuccessful hours of scaling over the jagged rock and dangerous precipices, without finding the little boy, the tired men were forced to give up the search. There was nothing more they could do.

The men regrouped at the foot of the mountain and along with the rest of the villagers discussed how they were going to break the bad news to the poor, panicked mother.

All of a sudden they looked up and, much to their great surprise, the mother was descending the mountainside with her boy clutched in her arms.

They were amazed! "How," someone asked her, "did you, being just a woman, find the boy after all the village's strongest men searched so hard and could not find him?"

She simply answered, "They aren't his mother."

A GOD THOUGHT

A man named Jerry Walker wrote some profound statements about the Father's all-sufficiency in our lives, no matter what we are feeling and experiencing. In the midst of loss of hope, faltering faith and a broken heart, God is speaking to each of us—giving us answers and reminding us of His promises and how He delights in us.

THE DESERTS OF LIFE

Ruined hope: deep pain; burning shame; shattered confidence; sickening despair; raw disappointment; paralyzing fear; terrorizing regret; mounting desperation.

Trembling faith: clinging to a thread of possibility; life closing in; cares and worries smothering;

burdens on overload and far beyond my strength.

Broken heart: struggling, trembling, faltering love; spoiled, ravaged self-image; tormenting thoughts; weariness almost unto death.

God's Answer: I Am Running to You

You are wondering or hoping or struggling to believe that I will welcome you? You say that you want My presence; you want My favor; you want to come back to Me? Listen to Me. My love for you has never faltered; I do favor you; I do desire you. I'm the One who knows you best and loves you most. I long to console you. I long to heal you. I long to renew your strength, give you a future and a hope and fill you with My joy. I have prayed that your faith will not fail, that hope will prevail—I will restore you.

But lift up your heart. As you struggle to turn around and take a feeble step toward Me, do you fear that I will turn My face from you? No, lift up your eyes and your heart—My arms are outstretched toward you. I am smiling and calling your name. My love for you is so unconstrained that I am even running to you.

His Promise: You've Gone to the Depths, but Now I Have Come for You

Don't turn back; keep walking toward Me. Yes, I know your weakness, devastation and selfish desperation. But I've been searching and calling for you. Now that you have begun, don't turn back.

My power will prevail. I am stronger than your heart; I am kinder than your thoughts; I am more tender than your pain.

I will hope for you; I will even believe for you; I will repeal your guilt and wretchedness; I will mend your broken heart; I will renew your mind; I will reclaim your liberty; I will restore your humanity; I will clothe you with dignity; I will rewrite your biography and reroute your destiny.

I will breathe new life into your crushed spirit, and power and soundness into your troubled mind. Here, give Me your trembling hand; I will take it and hold it close to My heart.

I will stay close to you—even when you feel far away.

His Delight: I Forgive You Freely, Quickly, Lovingly, Easily, Completely

Turn loose of all your condemnation, fear and despair, and take hold of My favor and delight in you.

This day I authorize you to live in My wholeness, My forgiveness, My liberty—enveloped in My love, overflowing with My abundance, delighting in close communion with Me.

You can trust Me to bring to perfection all that I love in you, all that I created you for, all that I've destined for you, all that I've known all along about you.

Your part in this, your place, is to believe in the One I have sent. Believe in My beloved Son and My presence with you by the Holy Spirit.

Should you waiver and stumble, quickly cry out to Me, "Father, I'm weighed down, and I'm slipping back!" I will hear your cry, help your unbelief and carry you in My arms.

From that resting place (whether in your believing or in My rescuing you from your unbelief), you can know Me more deeply, reach higher for all that I have for you, live life wider and give and receive love more fully.

Know this: I am rejoicing over you, My good creation, My redemptive handiwork, My blood-bought treasure, My child and heir to all that I have.

CHAPTER THIRTEEN

HE CHEERS FOR ME

*May our Lord Jesus Christ himself and God our Father,
who loved us and by his grace gave us eternal encouragement and good hope, encourage your hearts and strengthen
you in every good deed and word.*

2 THESSALONIANS 2:16-17

*"For I know the plans I have for you," declares the LORD,
"plans to prosper you and not to harm you, plans to give
you hope and a future."*

JEREMIAH 29:11

One of the things I love most about the Father heart of God is that He seems to always root for the underdog. I've always rooted for the underdog, too, probably because I always felt like one myself. Perhaps you, too, feel this emotion creep into your soul every now and then. Annie did. Read on to find out how her underdog status eventually led her to freedom in Christ.

Finding Freedom
By Annie Sanders

During the 1980s, most people would say that the Aiello family was the poster family for how to raise successful children. With two brothers attending the University of Notre Dame (one pursuing law; the other, medicine), another brother at Marquette University, a sister studying pharmacy to follow in her grandfather's footsteps, and the two youngest in private high school, we often were asked, "How do you do it?" Proudly, my father would answer, "If you work really hard, it will pay off." That's exactly what my father did. He worked really hard. Some would say he was a workaholic. As a realtor and a real-estate developer, Dad was rarely home during the week to spend quality time with my mom and us, except for running to and from our games and practices. He had to support a family of eight! While we all appreciated our dad being at our games, we all yearned for his attention when he was at home. I think part of the reason we excelled in what we did, both in the classroom and beyond, was partly to gain Dad's attention. Kids always want what they can't get, and so our excellent performance was one primary way of getting our dad's time and attention.

In 1983, my dad's real-estate development company folded because of severe recession conditions. Suddenly, the model for all of us to succeed changed. No longer was Dad able to financially support his children's attendance at private schools. And no longer was he able to give us his time. We sold our home and lake home and, to make ends meet, Dad took on multiple jobs. Suddenly, all of us were faced with the choice of paying our own college or high school tuitions or transferring to other schools. To add salt to the wound, my parent's relationship took a serious blow. After years of enduring a relationship kept alive by a thread, my parents struggled even more as the brief home time my dad had was now spent in an effort to keep our family from financial ruin.

Almost in an instant, our family went from have to have not. This placed unreal pressure on everyone in the family. After several separations, my parents divorced. Our family was supposed to be the poster family, but we were falling apart in front of our family and friends. We were failures before the public eye! We were not a "winning" family anymore, and it marked us all. Of all the children, the divorce affected Michael, the third eldest, the most.

More than any of us, Michael was the child who believed in the value of the family unit. He believed it was a good thing for Mom to be at home and Dad to be at work. When Mom had to go to work to help support her family, this was heart-wrenching for Mike. He wanted things the way they were. Michael was a perfectionist in every area of his life. If anything was out of sorts, out of place or lacked excellence, he would fix it. No matter how hard he tried, Michael couldn't fix this mess. When he realized there was nothing he could do to improve the situation, Michael took his own life. Michael's death was the numbing stab into the heart of our family. We died on October 29, 1983. Our family was no longer the same from that moment on.

Seven years after Michael's death, I accepted Christ as my Savior. On January 8, 1990, I realized there is a heavenly Father who knows me deeply. He knows my name. No longer would I need to work for the approval of my earthly father's attention. No longer would I need to prove my worth through my achievements or accomplishments. My worth lay only in the Father whose hand made me. Never again would I let perfectionism or accolades from people drive me.

The loss of my brother's life will always remind me that when things seem out of control, there is a Father who is in control and knows all my circumstances. This truth allows me to live in freedom.

I guess you could say that Annie and her family went full circle from most likely to most unlikely to succeed and then back again—for Annie—to finding her success and significance in the God who had made her.

I remember feeling as if everyone saw me as a "most unlikely to succeed" person. I was the last of six kids born into a middle-class family in El Paso, Texas, to Fred and Eileen Walker, on July 6, 1960. I don't know if it was because my other siblings constantly had opinions and things to say or if I just had a kind of out-of-the-womb shyness and insecurity problem, but my mom said I didn't speak until I was four years old. She even took me to the doctor to see if there was something wrong with me. I was so socially backward that I repeated kindergarten. This only confirmed some of my greatest fears that I wasn't sharp, that I was different and should just keep my mouth shut. I remember trembling with fear in grade school when a teacher would ask me to answer a question in front of the class. Needless to say, I was desperately shy and carried that behavior into my adulthood. I accepted the thought that no one would ever really want to hear what I had to say.

Before you start to feel too sorry for me, I did come from a loving home with an awesome Christian heritage, and I always felt loved and accepted.

My eleventh year was a big year for me. I accepted Christ (secretly praying the prayer every Sunday for several months just to make sure it took), started playing guitar and received my calling—all at about the same time.

I have always loved music, from my earliest memory. My mom plays the piano, and my whole family (though I think they were forced) would gather around and sing what I like to call "white gospel." It's not exactly the coolest musical background, but it's something I'm certainly becoming more and more thankful for. Many a night when I was just a little kid, I would crawl under my mom's baby grand as she played and fall asleep soaking in the sounds of the chords and melodies.

During the year I turned 11, there was a night I will never forget. The Christian band Love Song did a concert in my town. This band was among the very first Christian rock bands. After the concert, the band members came to my house for dessert. The next thing I knew, I was in my living room with all these guys, and Chuck Girard was at my mom's piano singing "Sometimes Hallelujah." I looked around at these traveling musicians who had given their gifts to God and thought, *That's what I want to be when I grow up!* Somewhere between my shyness—which made it easy for me to lock myself in my room and practice – and my determination not to give up and to serve God, I began my journey of serving Christ. By the way, later that same year, I wrote my first song. I put some Christian lyrics to a boogie-woogie progression I learned on the piano (not exactly the kind of thing that made anyone, even my mom, step back and take notice).

When I reminisce on those days, I certainly can't think of any reason why such a shy kid with bad grades and really no sign of extreme talent would wind up doing some of the things God has allowed me to do. In fact, from time to time, I have flashbacks and just laugh because I know it was only God's power working through me. I remember teaching a

---

IF YOU FEEL LIKE YOU'RE THE LAST ONE IN LINE, GOD IS ROOTING FOR YOU.

---

seminar from Jack Hayford's pulpit and thinking, *This is so unfair and ridiculous. Members of my family, my pastor and some of my other friends who are ministers are the ones who belong up here right now. They're the people with the real gifts.* And look at this, here I am writing a book when I so often battled with wondering if I would ever have anything of interest to say.

I tell my story to you for one reason and one reason only: If you feel like you're the last one in line, God is rooting for you. There are countless reasons why we all should be cut from the team—lack of ability, tragic circumstances or past sins—but our God loves a good comeback! How about the comeback of all comebacks—the Resurrection! God's strength is made perfect in our weakness (see 2 Cor. 12:9); He's the God of the second, third and hundredth chance!

One more thing: He's the redeemer. He redeemed my shyness and turned it into hours of practice. He can redeem your tragedies to give you insight so that you can bring God's hope and healing to people who are experiencing the same thing (see 2 Cor. 1:3-4). He even takes our sin and uses it to show us how desperate we are for the Cross and to warn others not to head into the same destructive ways.

For me, personally, this chapter delivers the most significant truth in this book. When I think of street children, orphans, the sick, the forgotten and the poor, and ponder how the Almighty doesn't forget about them or give up on them but believes in them and cheers for them, it makes me cry tears of joy. Think about it! God says the last will be first and the first will be last (see Matt. 20:16). This means that He will always make a place for people like you and me! I want to worship that kind of a God, don't you?

A God Thought

Everybody needs a cheerleader in this life. It is sad but true that many of you have never had one, and the only voices you hear from your past are the ones that say, "Don't even think about it;" "You could never do that;" "You'll never amount to anything." Stop! Wait! Listen to Me! These are not the voices of your God. These are the voices of the enemy who seeks to steal, kill and destroy every aspect of your life (see John 10:10). My perfect love believes all things and hopes all things (see 1 Cor. 13:7). In this race that you run, there will always be those who want you to lose and those who want you to win. Be reminded this day that your God is cheering for you and believing that you are going to win!

CHAPTER FOURTEEN

HE PREPARES A PLACE FOR ME

*Do not let you heart be troubled; believe in God, believe
also in Me. In My Father's house are many dwelling
places; if it were not so, I would have told you; for I go to
prepare a place for you. If I go and prepare a place for
you, I will come again and receive you to Myself, that
where I am, there you may be also.*

JOHN 14:1-3, *NASB*

*No eye has seen, no ear has heard, no mind has conceived
what God has prepared for those who love him.*

1 CORINTHIANS 2:9

At the end of the day, the only reason for us to feel any hope, purpose, love and joy is because we will forever be loved by the most powerful and important being in the universe—God Himself. We can only find true, authentic, long-lasting significance, acceptance and meaning in knowing that we are significant treasures to Him.

BECAUSE GOD HAS ALWAYS LOVED YOU LIKE NO OTHER WILL EVER LOVE YOU, HE CHEERS FOR YOU, BELIEVES IN YOU, WILL NEVER GIVE UP ON YOU AND IS PREPARING A PLACE FOR YOU!

Because God planned for you and made you, you can know that He wanted you. And if He wanted you enough to die for you, then you can rest assured that He has always loved you. And because He has always loved you like no other will ever love you, He cheers for you, believes in you, will never give up on you and is preparing a place for you.

What a God we have! What a hope we have! This earthly life is only a poor reflection, a foretaste, just a second in the whole of eternity of what lies ahead for us. Forever and ever, from the throne of our God, we will experience this kind of belonging, love and acceptance.

My Day Will Come
By Dan Glover

I was born the youngest of three boys to a young Pentecostal evangelist and his wife in the little "oil patch" town of Ponca City, Oklahoma, in the heart of Middle America. By the time I was five years old, I had traveled to 42 states and then moved lock, stock and empty barrel to the frozen frontier of Alaska. It was there that Dad and Mom began a ministry to military men who were constantly shipping out to Vietnam through Elmendorf Air Force Base and Fort Richardson in Anchorage, Alaska. In just a few years, I met hundreds of young men. A lot of them didn't come back from Vietnam, at least not alive. I remember hearing Dad call out their names in prayer, not knowing if we would ever see them again. Many of their names are memorialized on a huge black sheet of rock partially buried in ground in our nation's capital. I don't remember most of their names, but someone does. Someone misses each and every one of them.

After another few years, I became engaged to the lovely lady with whom I am so privileged to share my life. She just happened to be the daughter of my dad's best friend, so it was quite convenient; everybody already knew everybody else in the families. I had known her since she was four years old. Our happy parents decided to celebrate our engagement by taking a very long overdue vacation together. I saw them off at the Los Angeles airport with my young fiancée, after sharing our plans, hopes and dreams with them over Marie Callender's pie and coffee.

They visited places in Central America where Dad had preached as a young evangelist. They met old friends and made new ones on that trip. They traveled to many little towns and villages in the Mexican countryside. As they neared the end of their trip, they drove west out of Mexico City into the state of Jilotepec. A little after sunset, two men pulled alongside their car. One of the men held a handgun out the passenger window and shot my dad in the back of the head. He died instantly. The car was traveling more than 65 miles per hour and the ensuing single car crash was horrible. My mother was sitting in the right rear seat and was ejected out the driver's door with my dad's body. My father-in-law ended up between the passenger seat and the underside of the glove box. My mother-in-law ended up in the trunk of the car. Miraculously, only my dad died. The three survivors crawled away from the wreckage, wept over Dad and examined their injuries in the faint moonlight.

There are no words to describe the profound sense of loss we feel in such situations. I know that I will never forget the hours and days that followed that awful night. I will never forget the kindness of the Mexican people, the love of the local pastors or the many shared tears. My father-in-law preached the funeral, I sang "We Shall Behold Him," and I don't know how we made it through those days except that we were carried by friends and angels, all of them angels.

I married my lovely wife. Her father performed the ceremony. He had planned to share the moment with his best friend, but instead he remembered him. He preached a wonderful sermon, led us through our vows and we sang together as we left the service.

It is a great heaviness, a burden, if you will, to have so many good friends—the best of friends and family, the salt of the earth—precede me in death.

Years later, while serving as a sheriff, I was seriously injured in a confrontation with a person who had murdered three people. That injury resulted in pain that has been with me 24 hours a day for well over nine years now. It is pain that doctors compare with the pain of childbirth. It is pain that never changes, never ceases, never eases. It ended my career and ended life as I had known it.

I pray every day for release from this prison of pain. I wait patiently for relief to come. And I know that it will. It may come today. It may come tomorrow. It may never come in this life. But I know that one day, *one day*, it will be over. On that day, when I stand before my maker, when He calls my name, I will stand free from this pain. My pain is temporal, earthly, passing. It will not pass with me from this life to the next. Therefore, I must keep this view of life of constantly separating the temporal from the eternal. My pain and grief are of this world. My life is of another world.

It is with this perspective, this particular frame of mind, that I sat in a service at Christian Assembly and first heard Tommy sing these words:

I have a maker
He formed my heart

Before even time began
My life was in His hands

He knows my name
He knows my every thought
He sees each tear that falls
And hears me when I call

I have a Father
He calls me His own
He'll never leave me
No matter where I go

Yes, I do call on Him. I call and I cry every time I sing these words. You see, I have many, many friends who have gone before me. I know their names. I have an earthly father in heaven and a heavenly Father. They both know my name. My heavenly Father sees my every tear, and my earthly father will be there when I hear my heavenly Father call my name, when at last He will wipe away these tears that fall.

It is a beautiful, reassuring truth that God knows each one of us by name. He knows us intimately and has a redemptive purpose for each of our lives. In this last chapter, we contemplate the fullness of His marvelous plan—what He has in store for each of us for all eternity.

Many of the stories in this book speak about hardship, struggle and suffering. In fact, it is obvious that these true stories are not contrived or sugar-coated, because they openly and honestly talk about this earthly life's loose ends—all the ongoing troubles, unresolved problems and unanswered questions. Shining through it all is the beauty of the heavenly Father's loving intentions and redemptive purposes that ultimately will work for good for each and every one of us who trust Him.

And there's even more to come—much more. The Bible says, "Our present sufferings are not worth comparing with the glory that will be revealed in us" (Rom. 8:18). When we consider some of the tragic and intense suffering spoken of in this book and observe similar situations all around us in the world, it must be truly wonderful beyond our wildest dreams "what God has prepared for those who love him" (1 Cor. 2:9). It is a quantum leap into a reality not worth comparing with our present sufferings. What a future! What a hope!

God likes you *so much* that He's building you a house next door to His. It's not going to be your dream house, it's going to be beyond your wildest dream house. I have a hunch it will display all of your favorite colors and styles to reflect your individualistic tastes and personality. He's going to give you things to oversee that will fit your unique eternal design with unrestrained perfection. But even all of that will be nothing compared to those 1,000-year worship sessions at His feet.

The perfect way to end this book is to know His perfect ending. It is within our great, blessed hope and promise of eternity that every promise of God will finally be fulfilled. Until then there is no reason not to expect some sort of constant, undone longing in our hearts and lives until we are finally home.

If I had to sum up what the words "He knows my name" mean to me, it would go something like this: *Because I will forever matter to the One who matters most, nothing else really has to matter!*

A GOD THOUGHT

Ultimately, the Father heart of God will shine through and He will wrap His arms around each and every one of His children and carry them home to live with Him forever. A loud voice from the throne will say:

> Now the dwelling of God is with men, and he will live with them. They will be his people, and God himself will be with them and be their God. He will wipe every tear from their eyes. There will be no more death or mourning or crying or pain, for the old order of things has passed away (Rev. 21:3-4).

MINISTRY CONTACTS

Get Down Ministries
www.getdownministries.com

Get Down Ministries is a missions and worship resource ministry led by Tommy Walker under the umbrella of his church Christian Assembly of Eagle Rock, California. The goal of the ministry is to be a resource to the entire Church by providing anointed and inspiring worship music that will motivate the Church to passionately worship God and humbly reach the world. Profits from sales of the worship CDs fund the vision of worship evangelism around the world.

Caring@HelplessOnes.com

This e-mail correspondence ministry is provided for the encouragement of people who have a heart for the disabled and is focused on caregivers. E-mail responses include devotional thoughts and provide opportunities to correspond with others who face the challenges and blessings of ministering to disabled persons. E-mail addresses are not sold or distributed to anyone. A person may discontinue receiving messages at any time simply by e-mailing Caring@HelplessOnes.com.

Charlie's Lunch Ministry
www.charlieslunch.org

Charlie's Lunch Ministry began in 1997, when two street kids came begging for bread at Sam and Janey Stewart's door in Guatemala. The Stewarts, who were serving as missionaries at the time, were still grieving the loss of their little boy, Charlie, when the two street children came to the door. Janey decided to give these kids what she would have made Charlie for lunch. Soon the children and their siblings came every day to receive a lunch. Currently, Charlie's Lunch Ministry feeds 1,000 children on a regular basis, distributing nearly

10,000 meals each month in Mexico, Guatemala, El Salvador and India through Charlie's Lunch feeding centers. The children receive a hot, nutritious meal, hear a Bible story, sing songs and learn how important they are in God's eyes (and get a big hug from the director of the Charlie's Lunch feeding program). The mothers of the Charlie's Lunch kids volunteer to cook and serve the food and are also taught about the love of God. Many families have been added to local churches as this tool is placed in the hands of pastors and missionaries. Fifteen dollars a month can feed one hungry child through Charlie's Lunch Ministry. For more information, visit www.charlieslunch.org or call 915-584-1795.

HopeFinder.com

Hope Finder is an e-mail correspondence ministry to people who are experiencing depression and/or feelings of hopelessness. This ministry provides the opportunity to correspond with others in a similar situation who have found (or are finding) hope and victory and a way through the sadness and pain. E-mail addresses are not sold or distributed to anyone. A person may discontinue receiving messages at any time simply by notifying Hope Finder.

Live Worship with Tommy Walker

Featuring the song
"He Knows My Name"

New CD & DVD

Experience these amazing nights of **LIVE** worship
with gifted songwriter and worship leader Tommy Walker.

Find Tommy Walker music at
your local Christian Bookstore or Integritymusic.com

For more information on
Tommy Walker's ministry,
visit GetDownMinistries.com

Also Available in the Best-Selling Worship Series

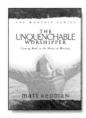

The Unquenchable Worshipper
Coming Back to the Heart of Worship
Matt Redman
ISBN 08307.29135

The Heart of Worship Files
Featuring Contributions from Some
of Today's Most Experienced
Lead Worshippers
Matt Redman, General Editor
ISBN 08307.32616

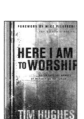

Here I Am to Worship
Never Lose the Wonder
of Worshiping the Savior
Tim Hughes
ISBN 08307.33221

Facedown
When You Face Up to God's Glory, You
Find Yourself Facedown in Worship
Matt Redman
ISBN 08307.32462